# *In the Arena*
# *of the Mind*

### Philippians 4:8

---

## John Vandegriff

A·S·K

Ask, Seek, and Knock Publishing
Howell, New Jersey 07731

**In The Arena Of The Mind**

Published by   Ask, Seek, and Knock Publishing
3071 Lakewood-Allenwood Rd.
Howell, NJ 07731

First Printing   May, 1992

---

**Publishers Cataloging in Publication Data**

Vandegriff, John
In The Arena Of The Mind / John Vandegriff

1. Christian life  2. Thinking  3. Spiritual renewal
I. Title
BV4501.2.V  1992   248.4 - dc20   92-070852
ISBN 0-9631725-0-6   8.95 Softcover

---

Calligrapher      Debi Paratore
Photographer      Dawn Marsh

*Printed in the United States Of America*

# TABLE OF CONTENTS

# FOREWORD

The "mind" is something Christians talk about but when pressed to define it, often find themselves hard-put to do so. Mind is not an entity, like a box or gland. It means me thinking. "Mind" speaks of the capability of the spirit to program the brain to operate the body. At death, the Bible tells us that mind ... the capacity to reason, self-consciously consider one's self, soliloquize and remember...survives. Mind, therefore, is inextricably bound up with the human spirit, which, as John Vandegriff shows, is the source of evil and good.

Prior to regeneration, the spirit could only program the brain to respond and to act sinfully. Since Christ freed us from the dominion of sin, Christians are now capable of doing good. But in this endeavor, a battle ensues. The body, habituated to sin, wants to continue in it. Habits are performed comfortably, skillfully, unconsciously and automatically. The spirit must reprogram the brain and through it, the members of the body, to live righteously (see Romans 6-8). But unless the mind is filled with new truths from Scripture, and until one begins to think God's thoughts after Him, the body cannot be reprogrammed for good.

John carefully pursues vital areas in which the mind must be renewed. He fills the book in simple language by interesting stories, with much helpful material for laymen and pastor alike. I hope it will be a blessing to many.

Dr. Jay E. Adams
*Harrison Bridge Road Associate*
Reformed Presbyterian Church
Simpsonville, South Carolina

# CHAPTER 1

# a penny for your thoughts

"Beware Of What You Set Your Mind On
For That You Will Surely Become."

Ralph Waldo Emerson

Your eyes are fixed and glazed, staring into space in unfocused blankness. You are drifting along in the warm reverie of a trance. Suddenly your serenity is shattered by, "A penny for your thoughts." Well, what have you been thinking? Are your thoughts worth a penny? Are the brain waves flat? Is your brain a place where sinful thoughts congregate? Or do thoughts that glorify God take root there, and later blossom into the fruit of the Spirit?

What is going on behind your eyes is of tremendous importance!

**The Importance of Thinking**

That thinking is a subject of great importance becomes clear when you see how often the words "mind", "thought" and "heart" keep cropping up in the Bible. There are well over one thousand such references. Thinking, therefore, is of critical importance to God. Although I'm sure I would have confessed that what we think about is very significant, yet, before I began to look into this subject, my own understanding was somewhat dim. I approached the subject tentatively, like a swimmer sticking his toe into water he supposes is icy. But the warm Biblical water teemed with passages that spoke of the mind. The more I searched, the more I saw that this is a vital subject - one which is near and dear to God's heart.

I saw that my thoughts are a primary gauge of the real me. Emerson said, "A man is what he thinks about all day long." The Bible puts it this way: "As he thinks within himself, so he is." (Proverbs 23:7 NASB).

The real person is the one inside the shell.  We can take all kinds of precautions to make sure the activities and exterior appearance are squeaky clean, but then if the thoughts are corrupt, the whole person is corrupt. Matthew records Jesus's hard words on this:

> "Woe to you, teachers of the law and Pharisees, you hypocrites!  You clean the outside of the cup and dish, but inside they are full of greed and self-indulgence. Blind Pharisee!  First clean the inside of the cup and dish, and then the outside also will be clean." (Matthew 23:25,26)

My wife and I have a cabin in the Catskill Mountains, and frequently we have visitors.  It is very interesting to see what treasures people leave behind.  One time after the cabin had been vacant for two weeks, my wandering eyes spotted a covered styrofoam dish - the kind that fast food restaurants put chicken in.  I opened it, and saw to my disgust that the two-week old chicken had become home to hundreds of creepy crawling things.  The outside of the covered styrofoam dish was clean and shiny; inside it was full of ugly white worms and rotten chicken.

The mind, a part of the unseen us, is a breeding ground for hypocrisy.  Ugly white worms of evil thinking can be eating away while the outside shell is smiling, doing good things, or carrying on sweet conversation.  Jesus makes it clear that we can appear to be one thing on the outside while the inside, unseen person is something else entirely.

It is easy to become quite expert at hiding that real but unseen you from other people.  Like an actor, you can always seek to present your best profile.  But there is also a very real danger that you might even deceive yourself. You convince yourself that because your external self looks good, all is fine.  Sometimes you don't even want to examine your own thinking much less open it up to the view of others.  It's easier to just block it out.

Larry Crabb emphasizes the need to concentrate on the inside,

> "The Bible speaks of wicked behavior as the outgrowth of a wicked and deceitful heart. The central problem is inside, within the heart. Effort will always be required to do what's right, but when we understand how to recognize and deal with sin in the heart, then the shift from sinful behavior to godly behavior will reflect an internal change that makes the shift real. 'First clean the inside of the cup and dish, and then the outside also will be clean.' " (Matthew 23:26)

One of the most searching passages in Scripture is Matthew 5:17-30. Jesus asserts that it is His purpose to fulfill the law not abolish it. He then makes the incredible statement that unless our righteousness exceeds the righteousness of the Pharisees (seemingly the most righteous people around) heaven was an impossibility. Talk about slamming the door of salvation! This would seem to nail it shut. But Jesus was saying that their standards, though outwardly impressive, were not high enough: they didn't take into account the inner person. Instead they shined and polished the exterior. Jesus then gives six examples of how attitudes are more important than externals, but the first two deal specifically with the workings of the mind.

Jesus places anger and murder in the same category (Matthew 5: 21-22). Thoughts of anger equal the act of murder. The Pharisees would claim "I'm o.k., I haven't murdered anyone." Jesus replies, "Yes, but if you've entertained angry thoughts about someone, you've killed him."

As if that wasn't enough, He states that the long, lingering, lustful look is equal to adultery (Matthew 5:27-28). Well, that shows that the Pharisee's standards were too low, but it also shows how important Jesus considers the mind to be.

Furthermore, the Bible makes it clear that proper thinking is fundamental for godliness. Notice what Paul says:

"Since, then, you have been raised with Christ, set your hearts on things above, where Christ is seated at the right hand of God. Set your minds on things above, not on earthly things." (Colossians 3:1-2).

These are the opening verses in a section that continues well into Chapter Four. This section teaches principles of godly living, but such living starts in the mind. The foundation for godly living is godly thinking.

Looking at it negatively, Jesus demonstrates the foundational relationship of thinking to godly behavior:

"For out of the heart come evil thoughts, murder, adultery, sexual immorality, theft, false testimony, slander. These are what make a man 'unclean';" (Matthew 15:19-20).

Evil actions arise out of the heart. The heart is the unseen part of us - our mind, will, and emotions. So the mind is where it all starts.

Charles Swindoll has said,

"Everyone I know who models a high level of excellence has won the battle of the mind and has taken the right thoughts captive."

Peter concludes his second letter in chapter three and verse one,

"Dear friends, this is now my second letter to you. I have written both of them as reminders to stimulate you to wholesome thinking."

Peter's purpose in both his letters was to stimulate wholesome thinking.

So it is a subject of major importance. One would think therefore that the bookstores would be full of great titles on thinking; that Christian authors would be cranking out all sorts of material on it. But the books are few and far between. Diligent inquiry turns up little.

So let's undertake this journey together. Our road will lead us to the desert of evil thinking. Although the view is ugly and depressing, it must be seen. Here we will learn to differentiate between sin and temptation. Next, the road will begin a 180 degree turn where we will learn how to stop evil thoughts and practice good ones. Finally, the road will climb through these dark clouds to the sunlit peaks where an extended study of each of the words in Philippians 4:8 will be described, practically applied, and contrasted with evil thinking. Here, and here alone, we can breathe the clean, pure mountain air.

# PART I

# IDENTIFYING AREAS OF SINFUL THINKING

*"The Thought of Foolishness is Sin"*

# CHAPTER 2

## thoughts that kill

"It's not what you eat,
it's what eats you."

Dr. S.I. Macmillan

The first area of sinful thinking to be identified is the thought of bringing harm. Hurtful thoughts are often retaliatory in nature. They may arise when someone has really committed an offense against me, or when I only imagine that they have. I think about how I might get back at them. This kind of thinking can occupy gigantic amounts of time and sour much of life. I can even get caught up in fantasy about what I might do if I got the chance.

**Everybody's Doin' It**

A few examples should help to show what this thinking is like, and why it is so bad. They will also demonstrate how common this kind of thinking is.

A few years before finding Christ, at Fort Dix in active training for the U.S. Army, I was involved in a rather complicated act of revenge. A somewhat frightened, bewildered, and a very uncomfortable group of young men had been gathered together and were asked if they had any R.O.T.C. experience. Although those courses were certainly not a highlight of my life, it still could be said that I had managed to pass the required two-year Reserve Officers Training Course; so my hand, along with a few others, tentatively rose into the air. There were, however, two hands that shot up with an air of great confidence. Now it is a law in the Army that you never volunteer for anything, but this was an exception to that rule because I was made an acting sergeant. The confident hands belonged to twin brothers who obviously wanted the authority that came with the R.O.T.C. experience. It soon became apparent that these two had no experience with anything to do with the Army.  It was also clear that they were power-crazy, and lorded it over their fellow recruits... These two facts, especially the latter, rankled almost every man in that platoon.  It became a rallying cry for us, "Wait 'til bivouac."

Bivouac is the reason many men don't like to camp.  It's that time when you do neat things like take 30-mile hikes with 35 pounds of stuff hanging off your body.  One of the things you carry is a nifty item called a shelter half.  This ingenious piece of equipment is a scrap of canvas that attaches to an identical scrap that your buddy has.  These two scraps make up a tiny pup tent that two adults can almost fit into.  Joyously, we discovered that the twins planned to share shelter halves.  An attack team had formed whose goal in life was to exact retribution upon these two interlopers.  Since they had made the Army life a good bit more miserable than it had to be, it became our happy duty to represent the rest of the platoon in getting even.  We, therefore, threw ourselves into the task with great glee.  Several sessions were held to develop a master plan.  On the second night of bivouac, while our enemies were peacefully sleeping, the team carried out its missions.  A deft pull of a cord collapsed the tent.  Ten helmets full of water were deposited on the former sleepers.  There would be little warmth the rest of that chilly spring night.  We marched across the pile several times as if for good measure.  As I look back on this, I shudder about the cruelty, but, you see, we had to get even.  After all, that's what the bumper sticker says, doesn't it?  "Don't get mad, get even."

The great national epidemic of divorce provides fertile ground for revengeful thoughts.  People plan and scheme how they can get back at former mates for all the suffering they went through in marriage.  One fellow, no doubt after many days of intensive hurtful thoughts, had his alimony payment delivered in large sacks of nickels. Another found a bank that made your own photographs a background for your checks. He had special checks made out for his alimony payments showing him passionately kissing his new wife.

Tony Campolo writes, "As I travel across America and talk to people, I realize how much pent-up anger there is in parents who have been humiliated and dealt with unjustly by their children. Everywhere I go, I sense in parents a repressed rage at children who talk to them in denigrating ways. Such parents feel most helpless when their children are too old to be punished, and so the anger builds up more." So it would seem that parenting provides grist for the mill of hurtful thoughts. I recently read a bumper sticker that said, "Get back - Live long enough to be a problem for your kids."

Evangelism Explosion, that fine evangelism program founded by D. James Kennedy, has a question in its gospel presentation that I've asked many times:

"If you were to die tonight, and you were standing before God, and He were to ask you, 'Why should I let you into My heaven?' What would you say?"

On several occasions, people have said, "I've never done anything to intentionally hurt anyone." This points out two things. One, is that they are probably depending upon their own good works for heaven, but it also shows that they don't have a good grip on reality. The fact is that everyone has purposely, knowingly, hurt others. We made our plan; we worked our plan; we rejoiced when our plan succeeded.

Yes, the sad truth is that we all spend precious time in the unprofitable activity of hurtful thoughts. Some will make plans of revenge. Some will just rehearse an argument over and over when the argument itself is over and all has been said. Yet, we still want to go over and over it until our stomachs are full of the black bile of bitterness.

**The Bible's View... These Thoughts are Murderous**

In the Sermon on the Mount, Jesus says,

> "You have heard that it was said to the people long
> ago, 'Do not murder, and anyone who murders will be
> subject to judgment.' But I tell you that anyone who is
> angry with his brother will be subject to judgment.
> Again, anyone who says to his brother, 'Raca,' is
> answerable to the Sanhedrin.  But anyone who says,
> 'You fool!' will be in danger of the fire of hell."
> (Matthew 5: 21,22)

Jesus had just said that He came to fulfill the law, and a
part of which is in the enlarging of the understanding of
the law.  "Kill" to the Pharisees meant the *act* of murder,
but Jesus expanded the meaning to include thoughts that
lead to murder.  He was talking about hurtful thinking.
    Let's take the statement, "Again, anyone who says to his
brother, 'Raca', is answerable to the Sanhedrin."  When
was the last time you saw something that made you mad,
and you hauled off and yelled, "Raca"?  Not lately, you
say?  Well, "Raca" is a word that means "emptyheaded".
Now that's more like the way we do talk and think.  When
was the last time you called someone "airhead," or ,
"stupid," or even "you jerk."  Imagine that you are driving
down a crowded highway trying to make good time.  All of
a sudden a car, which seems to personalize an arrogant,
nasty spirit, swerves into your lane forcing you to slam on
your brakes. What happens?  What words come to the tip
of your tongue?  What thoughts come to your mind?  Are
they at all similar to, "Raca"?
    Jesus' point is that we commit murder every time we
think that way.  But if that's murder, then I guess that it's
murder in the second degree; and I guess that the pre-
meditated, revengeful thinking that we often do would
have to be murder in the first degree.

## The Results of Hurtful Thinking

This kind of thinking produces some terrible results. Let me mention some.

The first one is that you cheapen yourself. When you want to get back at someone, you slide right down to their level. You end up in the same pit with them. John Edmund Haggai said,

"Let's go back to Abraham Lincoln for just a moment. While he was an occupant of the White House, some loquacious 'smut-sprayers' and 'character assassinators' spread the rumor that he was living with a black woman. What did the President do? Nothing. This man of poise had learned that in a fight with a skunk you might win the fight, but you will smell awful!"

The second result is that others get hurt. It isn't unusual for third and fourth, and sometimes many other parties, to get caught up in the storm. Not too long ago the newspapers were carrying a horrible story. A man who had been fired from an airline planned revenge on the boss who fired him. He was able to sneak a gun on board the plane his boss was on because he was familiar to the other employees. When the plane was aloft, he pulled out the gun. In the ensuing scuffle and wild shooting, the plane went down killing all aboard. Many innocent people were killed because of hurtful thinking that led to an act of violence.

More often, however, this result takes a more subtle form. There was a time when I was called into a situation where a woman's whole world seemed to be coming apart. After some probing, it came to light that an offense had been committed against her many years in her past. Pointing out the many verses that speak about Christian mercy, I pleaded with her to forgive the offender and leave the matter in God's able hands. She would have none of

it.  I had to watch helplessly as her bitter poison spread
from person to person in her family.  She hoarded the
hurtful thoughts as if they were some kind of treasure.  It
affected her disposition and even her countenance.  The
family was unable to overcome the daily contact with
bitterness, and they succumbed to unhappiness and
gloom.

A third result frequently comes as an unwelcome
companion to hurtful thoughts.  The thoughts are turned
inward and do tremendous damage.  The damage can be
felt physically and spiritually.

Let's look at the physical realm first.  There is almost
universal agreement that stress plays an important role in
physical illness.  Dr. S. I. McMullen, in his fine book,
None Of These Diseases, has a chapter entitled, "The High
Cost Of Getting Even."  It is a theme he keeps coming
back to again and again - stress hurts our bodies.  He
claims, for example:

> "Emotional stress can influence the amount of blood
> that flows to an organ.  Embarrassment can cause the
> blood vessels of the face and neck to open up to
> produce blushing, and the emotions of anxiety or hate
> can so increase the amount of blood within the rigid
> skull that headaches and vomiting result."

He adds,

> "Frequently, an emotional tempest sends S.O.S.
> messages to the thyroid gland for its secretions. When
> an excess of thyroxine is poured into the blood over a
> long period, the symptoms of toxic goiter are seen:
> extreme nervousness, bulging eyes, rapid pulse, and
> even fatal heart disease."

The adrenal glands are geared to respond to emotional
signals.  When my daughter Debi was just two years old,

my wife Ruthie, was doing some filing. The heavy metal filing cabinet tipped over and fell on Debi, who had pulled out the drawers below the one Ruthie was working with. Ruthie reached down, lifted the cabinet with one hand and with the other swept Debi out from under the filing cabinet, and then dropped the cabinet back on the floor. After comforting the dazed, bruised little girl, she reached down again to stand the cabinet back up; and although she was using all her strength, she was unable even to budge it. What happened? The adrenals had given her a momentary surge of power; the cabinet she had lifted with one hand later had to be made upright by two strong men.

These same adrenals which serve us so well in emergencies ooze out adrenaline when we become angry or hateful. Since there is no physical exertion, the oozing adrenaline becomes an oozing poison which hurts rather than helps the body. How sinful activity affects the body is a whole study in itself, but I have tried to shed a little light on what harm it can do. Yet, as bad as the physical problems are, I think that the spiritual problems are even worse.

Hateful thoughts directed at another person have a consequence on our own spirits. The Bible says, "Do not answer a fool according to his folly, or you will be like him yourself." (Proverbs 26:4 NIV). Certainly this verse tells us that if we get involved in an angry dialogue with an unreasonable person, we will become unreasonable.

The second part of that verse says that harboring hurtful thoughts about an unreasonable person can cause him to exercise control over you. It works like this. Suppose I'm a young woman all set to get married to the man of my dreams. The only problem is that my parents don't approve. But I go ahead and marry him anyway. Fully aware of their opposing opinion, I stubbornly strike out on my own, thinking, "I'll show them this is right." From that time on, I must prove that our marriage is right. Every time I wash a dish, I must do it better than my mother. I must keep the house cleaner. I must raise the kids better. In fact, *everything* I do has to be better. Well, then, what is the result? There is a strong negative attachment to my mother, and I am not free to focus my love on my husband. By way of her daughter's hurtful thoughts, that mother has become a dominating force in the life of her daughter, just the opposite of what the daughter intended.

Direct thoughts of enmity towards someone, and you invite that person to enter your life to dominate you. Rather than concentrating creatively on ways to better love those around us, we endlessly go over how we might have more perfectly squelched a comment. Instead of profitably designing methods to improve service for the Lord, we waste our creative juices fantasizing strategies to strike out at enemies, real or imagined.

We have examined the first area of sinful thinking - thoughts that kill. Now we'll go on to a second - self pity.

CHAPTER 3

The "Woe is Me" Syndrome

"I got gypped." High School Yearbook,
favorite saying of
John Vandegriff

When our yearbooks came out, like most people, I turned expectantly to the page where my own smiling face greeted me. What a surprise it was to find as my favorite saying, "I got gypped." "Do I really say that?" I asked. "Yeah, you sure do," I was told. It was quite a revelation. It made me take stock of myself. What I found was that I was a young man who lugged a duffel bag of self-pity around with me.

Because I had a very high opinion of myself, when I said that I got gypped, I was saying that I was such a great person that I deserved better. It was an expression of self-pity.

**Pity Your Local Prophet**

In 1 Kings 18 and 19, we have an amazing turn-around in the life of one of God's best servants, Elijah. In 1 Kings 18, we see him in overwhelming triumph. It's Elijah and God versus 400 prophets, the king and a skeptical nation. Man, he did it all! It was the prototype mountain-top experience!

But in 1 Kings 19, we see this brave man take flight at the threat of one woman. In his book on the life of Elijah A.W. Pink says,

"The contrasts presented by these chapters are sharp and startling. At the close of the one,'the hand of the Lord was on Elijah' as he ran before Ahab's chariot: at the beginning of the other, he is occupied with self and 'went for his life.' In the former, we behold the prophet at his best: in the latter, we see him at his worst.

There he was strong in faith and the helper of his
people; here he is filled with fear and is the deserter of
his nation. In the one, he confronts the four hundred
prophets of Baal undaunted; in the other, he flees
panic-stricken from the threats of one woman."

When his flight had taken him almost six weeks and
several hundred miles from Jezebel, he stopped for the
night in a cave. Then the word of the Lord asked, "What
are you doing here, Elijah?" His answer is a classic in the
literature of self-pity,

> "...I have been very zealous for the Lord God
> Almighty. The Israelites have rejected your covenant,
> broken down your altars, and put your prophets to
> death with the sword. I am the only one left, and now
> they are trying to kill me too." (I Kings 19:10)

Even as Job had his three friends to badger him in his
misery, so self-pity often has its three companions. They
are distortion, grumbling, and immobilization. For all
those days as he ran from Jezebel, Elijah had nothing to
occupy his mind but thoughts of self-pity. He lost his
view of reality. He thought that he was the only one
standing for God, when actually there were seven
thousand others.(1 Kings 19:18) He had even forgotten
that God plus one makes a majority.

And did he ever complain! Maybe he even dared to use
sarcasm with the Lord! You see, the name he used of God
contains the idea of the "Lord of Hosts". Does he dare to
call God that and yet claim that he is the only one over
whom God is host? Maybe yes, maybe no. But one thing
is for sure; Elijah practiced the age old art of griping.

Furthermore, it looks like his self-pity might have led to
immobilization of the worst sort - he would just as soon
die (v.4).

Let's look at these three evil companions of self-pity up close and personal.

### Fuzzy Thinking (Distortion)

The song says, "I can see clearly now the rain is gone." Self-pity, however, keeps us in a deep blue fog bank where we can't see clearly. Our view is distorted.

Paul speaks about this in Colossians 2:2,

> "My purpose is that they may be encouraged in heart and united in love, so that they may have the full riches of complete understanding, in order that they may know the mystery of God, namely, Christ,"

Here is the formula: Encouragement + Unity = Complete Understanding. So then to be encouraged leads to being able to see clearly. Is the converse true? Yes! The discouragement that walks hand in hand with self-pity leads to distortion.

It works sort of like a pair of binoculars. Look through them one way, and they seem to magnify. With self-pity, there's the tendency to magnify ourselves. Self-pity whispers about how wonderful you are, how good you've been, and how great your attitude is. And you know what? You believe it! If you take the binoculars and look through the wrong end, things look far away; and so it is with self-pity - you can hardly see the good in others, the good in your situation, even the goodness of God. Everything seems so far away.

With very few exceptions, people characterized by this see themselves as doing the best job humanly possible under the most trying circumstances. If that were not enough, they also seem blinded to any blessings that might be around, and this is what occupies their mind.

**Grousing, Griping, and Grumbling**

Self-pity can take total possession of thinking once it
gets a foothold in the brain.  A Christian leader that I
know recently shared with a group of us that during the
entire course of a twelve-hour drive, he had gone over and
over a small slight he had received at work.  He tried to
change his thinking, but he kept coming back as if
magnetically drawn.  I don't believe that is an unusual
experience.

As our cup is filled with these thoughts, the overflow is
what may be the real American pastime - griping.  In
Philippians 2:14-15, Paul makes some significant points
about complaining:

> "Do everything without complaining or arguing, so
> that you may become blameless and pure, children of
> God without fault in a crooked and depraved
> generation, in which you shine like stars in the
> universe..."

Note one thing that Paul talks about:  shining like stars
in the midst of a crooked and depraved generation.  It's
about how to be an "All-Star Christian."  You may not
have been an all-star at anything in your life, but you can
be an all-star at being a Christian.  "How?" you ask.  By
not complaining, Paul would answer.  Why is that?
BECAUSE EVERYONE GRUMBLES.  Just stand around
and listen, and you'll see that it's on just about every
tongue.  If you don't grumble, you'll stand out as one of
my friends put it, "like a shining star amidst the darkened
gloom of the grumbling gourmets."

Also, Paul states that you'll be blameless if you don't
gripe.  If someone were to complain about my lateness, I
would mentally check that someone out at the point of
their complaint.  "How is he in the area of lateness?," I
ask myself.  Since it isn't unusual to be very sensitive and,

therefore, very apt to gripe in the area of our weakness, my mental check-out often finds real fault. So the complainer lays himself open to countercharges.

I was asked to help a woman whose marriage was in deep trouble. Before I saw her, I asked her to write out a detailed description of the problem. I was not at all prepared for what I saw when we met. She placed a manuscript almost one inch thick before me and declared, "That's what the problem is." Now, I must admit that she had done that work for her lawyer in preparation for the impending divorce, but those chronicles of self-pity were right there in her memory just waiting to be dredged up. Self-pity had owned and operated her for some time. In fact that became abundantly clear the longer she talked. As bad as that husband might have been, her own thoughts seemed to be her worst enemy.

## Stuck In The Mud (Immobilization)

Something else that can develop as a result of self- pity is a kind of mental downward spiral. It works like this. Because these thoughts are sinful, guilt flows into my mind. Obviously, the proper response to guilt is to repent immediately. Often, however, that perverted inner nature of ours gets the upper hand, and we mentally jump right back in. After all, its such fun to have a real "pity party." Now guilt doesn't just go away; it gets worse. The thing grows within us like some science fiction monster. Depression rears its ugly head, and now we feel really bad - so bad we might stop doing things that we know that we ought to do. Of course, this makes us feel even worse. Talk about vicious cycles! This has got to be one of the worst.

This pattern happens regularly in some people who try to use it to their benefit. Chuck Swindoll describes them as "Poor Me Manipulators". He writes,

"This individual attempts to get his or her way by appearing weak. After all, who can hit you while you're down and helpless? These people 'clutch' at you, using sighs, tears, sickness, even depression to gain control and get their way. They love the role of victim, which seldom fails to arouse sympathy. Wives are great at this, so are kids! We can appear so needy, so ill...until we see it's not working."

There's a word to describe them, he says. It's "LONELY".

# CHAPTER 4

# The Paralyzing Thoughts - Fear

"For God did not give us a spirit of timidity, but a spirit of power, of love and self discipline." 2 Tim 1:7

Ever since I'd seen the opening scenes of a television series called, <u>Then Came Bronson</u> where Bronson rode a motorcycle on the incredibly beautiful highway which runs along California's Big Sur Coast, I had fondly wanted to drive that highway. My chance came during a family vacation several years ago.

The day was crystal clear as we left Carmel, heading South. Brilliant sun made the new vistas that greeted us at every turn all the more striking. We exulted in looking down on the beaches from soaring heights above. You see, I was used to the kind of beaches where you gaze out at the waves on their level, not looking down from lofty heights. Then almost without warning, we turned a corner and drove through a wall of fog. We went from dazzling sunlight to the gray-whiteness of a fog bank so thick the visibility was less than one hundred feet. The glittering sunlight was replaced by a dungeon of fog that held us prisoner for over one hundred miles. Gone was the joyous, carefree ride. In its place, was a tension-filled creeping ride, straining to see the center line of the road.

Well, worry is like that. When worry gets hold of you, it holds you in its gray grip. No longer is there a dazzling sun, only gloom. No longer are there spectacular views, only a compression brought on by the clouds of fear. Fog is not violent; it is with gentleness that worry surrounds and envelops you. Yet, like fog, worry can be lethal.

As we approach the issue of worry, it is important to point out that not all are under the spell of worry to the same degree. Some hardly worry at all, and others seem never far from it. I am one who seldom worries, but my wife, Ruthie, has struggled with worry all of her life. I used to kid her that heaven might be a dull place for her since she would have nothing to worry about. But she has had substantial victory over this unwelcome fellow traveler. Some of us need to understand others who worry more and some need to read the chapter in a self-applicatory way.

My task will be to carefully examine worry. We'll seek out a biblical definition of worry and also look into the results of worry.

## Worry - What It Is

Two concepts, coming from the New Testament words, form our idea of worry.

The first of these is found in Matthew 6:34,

"Therefore do not worry about tomorrow, for tomorrow will worry about itself. Each day has enough trouble of its own."

The word used for worry in the original is a compound word, the first part of which means 'divided' and the second 'memory' or 'mind.', so it comes to mean a divided mind.

John Edmund Haggai, picking up on this theme, writes:

"Worry, then, means 'to divide the mind.'
Worry divided the mind between worthwhile interests and damaging thoughts...
Peace of mind requires a singleness of mind. The worrier robs himself of peace of mind by dividing his mind.
Worry divides the feelings, therefore the emotions lack stability.
Worry divides the understanding, therefore convictions are shallow and changeable.

Worry divides the faculty of perception, therefore observations are faulty and even false.

Worry divides the faculty of judging, therefore, attitudes and decisions are often unjust. These decisions lead to damage and grief.

Worry divides the determinative faculty, therefore, plans and purposes, if not 'scrapped' altogether, are not fulfilled with persistence.

Worry in the extreme leads to abulia, 'loss of the power to will.' Why? The mind is so divided it cannot act in one channel. It is like the mule who stood between two haystacks and starved to death trying to decide from which stack to eat."

The second concept is fear. The New Testament word, PHOBOS from which we get our word phobia, in addition to the reverential fear of God, means plain old terror.

Fear is the foundation upon which the gloomy house of worry is built. Jay Adams incitefully writes:

"Love looks for opportunities to give; it asks: 'What can I do for another?' Fear keeps a wary eye on the possible consequences and asks: 'What will he do to me?' Love 'thinks no evil'; fear thinks of little else. Love labors doing today's tasks and is so busy that it has no time to worry about tomorrow. Because it focuses upon tomorrow, fear fails to undertake responsibilities today. Love leads to greater love - fulfilling one's obligations brings joy and peace and satisfaction and greater love and devotion to the work. Fear, in turn, occasions greater fear, since failure to assume responsibilities brings additional fear of the consequences of acting irresponsibly.

Love is self-giving; fear is self-protecting.

Love moves toward others; fear shrinks away from them."

From Adams' contrast of love and fear, we can learn much about worry. Worry keeps a wary eye on possible consequences. Worry thinks about all the dark possibilities of a situation. Worry, like self-pity, can be so focused on tomorrow (all the things one can't control), that it fails to undertake today's responsibilities.

As we complete our look at what worry is, let me zero in on one of Adam's statements which is:

> "Fear, in turn, occasions greater fear, since failure to assume responsibilities brings additional fear of the consequences of acting irresponsibly."

Worry escalates. The worried thinker imagines all sorts of bad things. There is a kind of "what if" mentality. A "good" worrier might even run a pattern like this:

Thought #1:     "My son is late."
Thought #2:     "What if he had an accident?"
Thought #3:     *(comes as the exercised imagination of the professional worrier comes to life.)* "What if he is paralyzed for life?"

Then come the questions: "What will I ever do? How will we ever care for him?" etc., etc.

Now that we have looked at what worry is, consider wounds that worry inflicts on those who practice it.


**Worry - The Wounds It Inflicts**

The first wound is physical. In <u>None of these Diseases</u>, Dr. S.I. McMillen gives this brief case history:

> " '(Doctor, I came to you because I am all tuckered out. Before this thing hit me, I could work all day and

not be tired. Now, when I start across the field on the tractor, I get so weak that I stop before I get halfway across. I have to get off the tractor and lie down by the fence before I get strength to go on. That's not like me. For the past month, I have been completely bushed. I have been losing weight too.)'

I stared in amazement at a husky, twentyyear-old farmer. He was the type who was never sick, yet here he was wholly incapacitated for work. My first thoughts were of severe anemia, leukemia, or perhaps internal bleeding. The possibility of cancer and tuberculosis came to my mind. However, a physical examination and laboratory tests showed no organic trouble.

I questioned the young man more carefully. I discovered that his attractive fiancee was doing a little dating with another lad. Also, a man who had promised to give him a good bargain on a used car had now raised the price two hundred dollars. The fear of losing both girl and car had been causing my patient to lose his appetite, his sleep and his strength.

Yes, this unusual fatigue was entirely due to worry and anxiety. Dr. Hans Selye, a world authority on stress, has shown that long and continued stress results in exhaustion. Not work but worry makes us weary. Explaining the situation to my patient and giving him a few sedative tablets did the trick. His normal strength came back and even his appearance improved so much that he won and married the girl of his choice.

This finding is confirmed by recent medical studies.

A story in USA TODAY reads,

"Chronic fatigue may be more common and more crippling than we think.".

And it's more often tied to depression or anxiety than to physical illness, says a study in today's Journal Of The American Medical Association.

One in four patients - 276 of 1,159 - studied in two
San Antonio Clinics reported fatigue lasting at least a
month. Average duration: three years.

The duration and severity of the fatigue surprised
study author Dr. Kurt Kroenke, Brooke Army Medical
Center, Fort Sam Houston, Texas. 'Chronic fatigue is
often dismissed as a minor complaint,' he says. But
patients' perceived disability (was) like that of patients
recovering from major illness such as heart attack.'

Kroenke's team tested 102 patients. Lab tests turned
up no unsuspected physical causes for fatigue, but 80
per cent had abnormally high scores for depression or
anxiety, manifested in symptoms such as tension
headaches, and dizziness.

After tests for physical causes, doctors should
consider emotional factors including stress, depression
and anxiety, he says."

McMillen also connects worry with arthritis. In Stop
Worrying and Get Well, Dr. Edward Padolsky
demonstrates a correlation between worry and heart
trouble, high blood pressure, some forms of asthma,
rheumatism, ulcers, cold, thyroid malfunction, arthritis,
migraines, blindness, and most stomach disorders in
addition to ulcers.

John Edmund Haggai writes:

"There are some outstanding young doctors who
have founded and who staff the Medical Arts Clinic in
Corsicana, Texas. Two of these, a brilliant young
surgeon by the name of Louis Gibson and a sharp
young internist by the name of Robert S. Bone, told me
recently that the first complaint of more than 70 per
cent of the people coming to them is, 'Doctor, I can't
sleep,' Why? Worry!"

Worry wounds leave significant physical scars. And yet some unseen wounds that scar the soul of a person may be even worse. Let's look at them.


## A Dark Outlook

Since a worrier tends to see things in their worse possible light, worry can develop into full-blown pessimism. Now, seeing problems can prevent one from falling into unnecessary difficulties. Caution is good when it causes one to consider potential pitfalls that need to be overcome or even when it puts the brakes on a project that is overly dangerous. But sinful worry can cause a dark outlook which sees only the downside of things.

The story is told that two men were talking about their bird dogs. "Have you seen my new dog? He's the best money can buy," one man said.

The other replied, "He doesn't look so hot to me."

The new owner proposed that they go hunting so that he could prove the tremendous value of his new dog, and it was arranged. Shots rang out, and ducks fell from the sky into the pond. The new owner ordered his dog to get the ducks, and he responded by sprinting across the surface of the water, retrieving the ducks and bounding back on the top of the water.

A smile of satisfaction spread across the face of the new owner as he asked, "What do you think of that?"

His pessimistic friend replied, "Hmmm, can't swim, can he?"

Thus, people consumed by worry can develop a dark outlook; but there's more.

## A Disorganized Mind

Much like self-pity, worry can have a debilitating effect. Afraid to make a move for fear of what might happen, a strange immobilization can develop.

Imagine a person who is fearful in the midst of a busy day. "What will I do?" he asks himself. I can't follow option A because this, that or the other thing might happen. I can't follow option B because of similar possible difficulties. This is the situation that is described so well in James 1:6-8,

> "But when he asks, he must believe and not doubt, because he who doubts is like a wave of the sea, blown and tossed by the wind. That man should not think he will receive anything from the Lord; he is a double-minded man, unstable in all he does."

No matter what the inveterate worrier thinks about, there is fear-based doubt which makes decision-making hard, if not impossible. It reminds me of the squirrel that darts one way and then the other as your car approaches. If he goes either way decisively, he'll be okay, but sometimes he can't decide and pays for it with his life.

An organized person sees what he must do, settles on a plan of attack and goes for it. A worrier frequently can't decide what plan to follow and is, therefore, disorganized.

But as bad as all this may be, the worst is yet to come.

## A Distrust In God

Frequently worry is saying no to the promises and commands of God. For a professing Christian, this amounts to hypocrisy. A Christian claims to trust Christ, but to worry is to deny Christ's promises.

I like the saying, "Worry looks around, but faith looks up.". This sums it up, doesn't it? While the Bible triumphantly states, "I can do everything through him who gives me strength." (Philippians 4:13). The worrier looks around shooting holes in that promise and, in effect, calls God a liar. Whereas David, inspired of the Spirit said, "The Lord is my shepherd, I shall not lack,", the worrier looks around for instances when things didn't go as he wanted.

I John 5:10b says,

"Anyone who does not believe God has made him out to be a liar, because he has not believed the testimony God has given about his Son."

Incredibly, there are many who, by worry, make God out to be a liar. What could be worse?

So we have examined worry as to its description and devastating results. Now, let's turn to another sinful way of thinking.

# CHAPTER 5

"GIMME, GIMME, GIMME"
"you've only got one trip
through this world, you've got
to grab all the gusto you can."
1960's beer ad

Sometime ago, there was a tremendous turmoil over a movie entitled, The Last Temptation of Christ. Among several points of controversy is a scene where Jesus fantasizes on the cross what married life would be like and even dreams of sex with Mary Magdalene. Some say,"Blasphemy!" Others soothingly reply, "No, this just shows Jesus' humanity; it clearly brings out that He struggled just as we do." It is true that Jesus was tempted at every point as we are. Hebrews 4:15 tells us this. Also the Gospels record the threefold temptations of Jesus and His victorious resistance of them. Yes, Jesus was fully human, was tempted but did not sin!

James says,

"...but each one is tempted when by his own evil desire, he is dragged away and enticed. Then after desire has conceived, it gives birth to sin; and sin, when it is full-grown, gives birth to death." (James 1:14-15)

Temptation comes as a thought. When the thought flashes into our minds, it is only a temptation. James says the thought comes from our own evil desire (lust) and can drag us away. Desire conceives and gives birth to sin. Temptation becomes sin when we dwell on it in our minds. If I erase the thought off the blackboard of my mind the moment it appears, I've been tempted, but I've evaded sin. If I dwell on the thought, I am dragged away by the temptation, and it becomes sin. The Chinese proverb sums it up: You can't stop the birds from flying over your heads, but you can stop them from building a nest in your hair."

So many say that <u>The Last Temptation of Christ</u> only depicts temptation that Christ went through. But Jesus Himself said,

> "You have heard that it was said, 'Do not commit adultery.' But I tell you that anyone who looks at a woman lustfully has already committed adultery with her in his heart." (Matthew 5:27,28)

Jesus is plainly saying that to fantasize sex with a woman is sin. Clearly then, <u>The Last Temptation of Christ</u> portrays not temptation, but sin.

## Lustful Thinking

We come now in our delineation of sinful thought patterns to that wicked, but common pattern, lustful thinking. The Greek word translated "lust" means a very strong desire for something, whether good or bad.

You can "lust" after God, and this is, of course, very good. However, often in the Bible the object of lust is something evil. The English word seems always to have this latter meaning. Furthermore, lust usually is a strong desire for something for yourself. It is a taking to oneself. This taking to oneself can be sexual in nature, or lust for material things.

The temptation of Eve is described in Genesis 3:6,

> "When the woman saw that the fruit of the tree was good for food and pleasing to the eye, and also desirable for gaining wisdom, she took some and ate it."

The connection can be made to I John 2:15-16 which reads,

"Do not love the world or anything in the world. If anyone loves the world, the love of the Father is not in him. For everything in the world - the cravings of sinful man, the lust of his eyes, and the boasting of what he has and does - comes not from the Father but from the world."

The King James Version has it very literally, "the lust of the flesh, the lust of the eyes and the pride of life."

| Genesis | John |
|---|---|
| Good for Food | Lust of the Flesh |
| Pleasing to the Eyes | Lust of the Eyes |
| Desirable of Gaining Wisdom | Pride of Life |

Lust of the eyes is: I see it and I want it. At this stage, it hasn't gone past the mind. Jesus said,

"You have heard that it was said, 'Do not commit adultery.' But I tell you that anyone who looks at a woman lustfully has already committed adultery with her in his heart." (Matthew 5:27,28).

So Jesus makes it plain that the lust of the eyes (thinking) which leads to the lust of the flesh (doing or fulfilling the desires) is sinful. It is a sin in the mind.

This is exactly what happened to David. It is there for us to read in 2 Samuel 11. When he saw the beautiful Bathsheba, he wanted her; he lusted after her. This is lust of the eyes. It became lust of the flesh when he committed the act with her.

**A Description of Lust**

I suspect we know lust far too personally to need a great deal of description, but perhaps elaboration will help us to see what a horror lust really is.

**Lust Is Common**

Lust is common. There a common cold and a common house fly. So being common can be bad enough. In an excellent chapter on the subject of lust, Anthony Campolo writes on the commonness of this sin of the mind:

> "There was a time when I would have pretended that such was not the case (that Christians have lustful thoughts). I was sure that the other Christians I knew would be shocked and break fellowship with me if they knew what went on in my mind. Those in the church seemed beyond lustful fantasies which plagued my consciousness. However, I have since learned that I am not the only one in the church who, from time to time, fantasizes about the possible joys of sexual liaisons. In the words of one preacher: 'It's depressing to realize that most of us are like the rest of us!' The problem with lust is common to all who live this side of Eden."

It has been my experience that when people get honest about what is really going on in their lives, lust is common. There are those who would have you believe that an impure thought never comes into mind; but sometimes after a little coaxing, even they will admit that they fight against these thoughts.

**Lust Is Immature**

Love and lust are opposites. The Scripture points out that love is giving. Lust is taking. After showing the necessity of love and description in I Corinthians 13, Paul notes love's unfailing character. In the midst of this description, he says in verse 11,

"When I was a child, I talked like a child, I thought like a child, I reasoned like a child. When I became a man, I put childish ways behind me."

Love, then, is a mature thing. Paul says when he grew up, he put away childish things. He put away the childish ways of thinking, including lust. This he sees as being immature.

The immaturity of lustful thinking can be seen in the person who always thinks "the grass is greener in the other pasture." It may be someone else's car, job, or wife. It may be a Christian who looks at another church. He looks over and says, "They don't have brown spots that I've got in my pasture," so he jumps the fence. And what does he find? There are almost as many brown spots as there were in his old pasture. What's the problem? He overestimated what he didn't have. He thought the next field was better than it really was. He also underestimated the field he was in. It wasn't as bad as he had thought. His view of reality was distorted.

So it is with lustful thinking. Lust sweeps away realistic views. The thing you want so desperately isn't all you think it is, and the thing you have isn't so bad.

**Lust is Selfish**

This seems obvious. Lust is taking for myself, so it has to be selfish. In fact, this is selfishness in its most basic form.

Jesus' parable in Luke 12:16-21 is instructive.

"The ground of a certain rich man produced a good crop. He thought to himself (Note how often its in the mind), 'What shall I do? I have no place to store my crops.' Then he said, 'This is what I'll do. I will tear down my barns and build bigger ones, and there will I

store all my grain and my goods.' And I'll say to myself,
'You have plenty of good things laid up for many years.
Take life easy; eat, drink and be merry.' "
    But God said to him, 'You fool! This very night your
life will be demanded from you. Then who will get
what you have prepared for yourself.' "

Charles Swindoll comments on this,

    "He didn't really care about other people. His
    remarks are thoroughly, completely, unashamedly full
    of himself. He is occupying the throne of his own life.
    In the English version of my Bible, I count six 'I's' and
    five 'my's. Never once do we find 'they', 'them', and
    'their'. He cares only about 'I', 'me', and 'my'. Greed
    personified. William Barclay writes: 'It was said of a
    self-centered young lady, 'Edith lived in a little world,
    bounded on the north, east, south and west by
    Edith.' "

Isaiah says,

    "The scoundrel's methods are wicked. He makes up
    evil schemes to destroy the poor with lies, even when
    the plea of the needy is just." (Isaiah 32:7)

Again, it is the mind that makes up evil schemes. The
schemes are at bottom lustful, selfish thoughts. To get
what he wants, the scoundrel walks over those with real
needs.
A business newspaper showed a business organization
chart with men with suits and briefcases in the little
boxes. It showed two men going for one higher position,
and finally only one reaching the pinnacle. The young
business lions are told that with this newspaper as a tool,
they can make it to the top. In America, we seem to lust

for the top and it's O.K. to put our boot on the face of anyone in our climb up there.

Well, it's pretty gruesome, isn't it. The picture doesn't get any prettier as we look at the results of lustful thinking.

## The Results of Lust

As with other kinds of sinful thinking, thoughts of lust have inevitable results. These results are devastating and should cause us to be careful not to lapse into lustful thoughts. Here are some that I have observed.

## Lust Doesn't Satisfy

Solomon gives us true wisdom when he says in Ecclesiastes 5:10, "Whoever loves money never has money enough; whoever loves wealth is never satisfied with his income." There it is! If I lust after something, when I get it, I'm not satisfied. Then I need something else, something more. How many times have I wanted something so bad I could almost taste it? The almost overwhelming desire to have it dominated my thinking. Then the day came when I possessed it. There was an immediate and powerful flush of happiness, but it soon disappeared down the drain. It wasn't long before I wanted something else.

Not long ago, a stereo we had had for years was breathing its last feeble breaths. I began to check out catalogs. The more I looked, the more I wanted. I found a system I liked, and the desire increased geometrically. The day I brought it home, I spent hours listening to old albums. But the pleasure I get from it now is disproportionately small compared to the desire I had before purchasing it.

Years ago, the sales slogan for a particular brand of cigarettes was, "They satisfy." If they satisfied, one would think that one cigarette would do it. There would be everlasting contentment. But anyone who smokes knows that very soon satisfaction gives way to the need for another cigarette.

Sexual lust operates on this principle. People caught up in lust need to get progressively perverse in their sexual activity. Since lust gratification is not really satisfactory, the kicks have to be different and greater, more and more perverse. Then comes the time when even the perversion doesn't gratify. The sad fact is that lust simply doesn't deliver.

## Lust Brings Misery

The second result of lustful thinking is that it brings misery.

James wrote,

> "Now listen, you rich people, weep and wail because of the misery that is coming upon you. Your wealth has rotted, and moths have eaten your clothes. Your gold and silver are corroded. Their corrosion will testify against you and eat your flesh like fire. You have hoarded wealth in the last days." (James 5:1-3)

In an article by Jim Spense about the life of Howard Cosell, this principle seemed to be true in Cosell. The following is taken from TV Guide, June 4, 1988:

> "Howard Cosell had begun to change in the mid-'70's and eventually he actually became a different person from the one I had known originally. The bigger his celebrity, the greater his insecurity. I can say this without hesitation: In the later years of our

relationship, Howard Cosell turned into one of the most insecure human beings I have ever met. And, for the life of me, I don't know why. Here was a man, a very moral man, a solid family man who had a deep and secure and loving relationship with his wife, Emmy. He had two daughters and four grandchildren whom he cherished. He was bright, articulate, successful and recognized beyond his wildest imagination. He deserved tremendous credit for contributing enormous amounts of time to many charitable causes, for which he received deep appreciation. He had made millions of dollars, traveled the world, been applauded and honored time and time again. Yet, today, I think he is one of the unhappiest human beings on this planet. Instead of enjoying his success, he let it devour him."

It seems that lustful thoughts played a big part in his misery. So it is with us all. Since lust doesn't deliver what it promises, all our thoughts and efforts bring misery rather than satisfaction. It is this very lack of satisfaction that is so miserable.

## Lust Leads Away From The Faith

Two passages demonstrate this. First, we will examine Matthew 6:19-24:

"Do not store up for yourselves treasures on earth, where moth and rust destroy, and where thieves break in and steal. But store up for yourselves treasures in heaven, where moth and rust do not destroy, and where thieves do not break in and steal. For where your treasure is, there your heart will be also.
The eye is the lamp of the body. If your eyes are good, your whole body will be full of light. But if your

eyes are bad, your whole body will be full of darkness. If then the light within you is darkness, how great is that darkness!

No one can serve two masters. Either he will hate the one and love the other, or he will be devoted to the one and despise the other. You cannot serve both God and Money."

This passage states that one mastered by lust for money can't also serve God as Master. If you come to the fork in the road and choose lust for money, the further you go down that road, the further away you get from God.

But even more explicit is I Timothy 6:10,

"For the love of money is a root of all kinds of evil. Some people, eager for money, have wandered from the faith and pierced themselves with many griefs."

Here wandering and lusting are linked together as cause and result.

I had a ministry with a woman I'll call Doris who had a struggle with anxiety. When she looked to Christ for help, she experienced significant victory over anxiety. For some time, she seemed to seek the Lord, but I noticed that material things became increasingly important. In order to pay for all the stuff, she took on one, and then another job. Her relationship with the Lord cooled, and she became less and less involved in the church, until we just didn't see her anymore.

I have known many kids who were seemingly red hot for Jesus until they approached the age for the driver's license. That is the time of life when thoughts turn to cars. They must work to support the car. The same person that would have never missed a Youth meeting is soon a missing person whose hands can't be pried loose from the steering wheel. Their love of things is more evident than their love for the Lord.

It is a grim picture, isn't it?  Yet, there is one more area of sinful thinking.  Let's proceed on to it.

# CHAPTER 6

# the single "I"

"pride goes before destruction,
a haughty spirit before a fall."
proverbs 16:18

Anthony Campolo tells this story in his excellent chapter on pride in his book Seven Deadly Sins:

"Savonarola, the great Florentine preacher of the fifteenth century, one day saw an elderly woman worshipping at the statue of the Virgin Mary which stood in his city's great cathedral. On the following day, he noticed the same woman again on her knees before the Blessed Mother. With great interest, Savonarola observed that day after day, she came and did homage before the statue.

'Look how she reverences the Virgin Mother,' Savanarola whispered to one of his fellow priests.

'Don't be deceived by what you see,' the priest responded. 'Many years ago an artist was commissioned to create a statue for the cathedral. As he sought a young woman to pose as the model for his sculpture, he found one who seemed to be the perfect subject. She was a young, serenely lovely woman, and had a mystical quality in her face. The image of that young woman inspired his statue of Mary. The woman who now worships the statue is the same one who served as its model years ago. Shortly after the statue was put in place, she began to visit it and has continued to worship there religiously ever since.' "

This is an extraordinary example of self-worship! Although this is flagrant, I think all of us have become experts in more subtle forms of self-worship. Campolo defines pride as "arrogant self-worship." I would offer also the idea of wanting to be somebody. Pride is wanting to rise above my fellows.

The camera sweeps the crowd. They all have their index fingers held aloft. They scream, "We're number one." That scene is reenacted often in places other than the athletic arena. When I want to rise above others so that I may receive glory for myself, that's pride.

## Raising the Banner of My Name

Proud thinking may be described as scheming to make a name for ourselves. Genesis 11:1-9 tells of the building of a huge tower. Why did they build it? Was this building erected to the honor of God? Was it a temple for worship of the Almighty Creator of the Universe? No! The builders and designers proudly said,

> "Come, let us build ourselves a city, with a tower that reaches to the heavens, so that we may make a name for ourselves and not be scattered over the face of the whole earth."

They wanted to raise a tower to honor their own name. The problem is we do it too. We fill our minds with plans of projects to enhance our own reputations. I wonder, "How can I look better? Ah, here's a way." Then I hone and sharpen the plan. That's proud thinking!

We need to be careful at this point to differentiate between giving the very best effort with the gifts God has given us for His glory and giving our best effort for our own glory. The former is right and proper. It is God-honoring. The latter is building a tower of Babel.

### Fill'er Up With Self

Picture yourself at a self-service gas station.  Only instead of gas you're pumping high octane self into your tank.  Simone Byers tells this story:

> "My dad operates a small business and is always looking for new ways to make money.  His ingenuity worked overtime once when he remarked about an egotistical customer:  'I'd love to buy that guy for what he's worth and sell him for what he thinks he's worth!'"

Well, here was a guy that had pumped himself full of self.

There are three occasions Jesus spoke to full-of-self people.  The first is in Luke 18:9-14:

> "To some who were confident of their own righteousness and looked down on everybody else, Jesus told this parable: "Two men went up to the temple to pray, one a Pharisee and the other a tax collector.  The Pharisee stood up and prayed about himself; 'God, I thank you that I am not like other men - robbers, evildoers, adulterers - or even like this tax collector.  I fast twice a week and give a tenth of all I get.'
>
> "But the tax collector stood at a distance.  He would not even look up to heaven, but beat his breast and said, 'God, have mercy on me, a sinner.'
>
> "I tell you that this man, rather than the other, went home justified before God.  For everyone who exalts himself will be humbled, and he who humbles himself will be exalted.' "

Notice that in verse 9 Jesus says the Pharisees were confident of their own righteousness and looked down on everybody else.  They were full of pride.  The parable

shows that these people count all they do to be good.
They don't see their sin, shortcomings, or need.

The second is Revelation 3:17 where Jesus has John
write to the Laodicean church,

> "You say, 'I am rich; I have acquired wealth and do
> not need a thing, But you do not realize that you are
> wretched, pitiful, poor, blind and naked."

They thought they were so great, but didn't realize how
bad off they were. They were like a young athlete friend of
mine of whom it was said, "He doesn't need a fan club;
he's got himself."

The third is found in John 8:37. John 8:31-59 reports a
discussion between Jesus and some Jews who were
friendly to Him and believed in Him to some extent --
though not savingly. He reproaches them in verse 37,

> "I know you are Abraham's descendants. Yet you are
> ready to kill me, because you have no room for my
> word."

Jesus tells them that the truth will make them free, and
they want to kill Him. That is pride! They hear that they
have needs, and they want to strike out and kill. They
were so full of themselves that they had no room for His
Word.

Now, how does this pride that makes me full of myself
affect my thinking? First, because we think so highly of
ourselves, we make excuses for ourselves. We rationalize
sin and mistakes. One time I asked a couple who were
struggling in their marriage each to write out a list of very
specific ways in which they sin against the other. I took
care to explain what I meant. They repeated what they
understood me to mean, and went off to do their work.
When they returned, one had written down things like, "I

am too forgiving," and "I am too honest." She was excusing herself and didn't see her sin.

Adam did it, too. When God questioned him, he pointed at Eve and then at God, "The woman you put here with me - she gave me some fruit from the tree and I ate it." (Genesis 3:12). It might be interesting for you to count the number of times you excuse yourself, or shift the blame, in one day.

How often I have gone over situations in my mind and mentally defended myself. This is proud thinking! The worst time for me is when I have had an argument. It's passed, but I go over and over it trying to sharpen what I could have said. Why, that's nothing but uncrucified, unadulterated pride! Not only that - it is a complete waste of time, a totally unproductive use of the mind.

**The Foundation of Sinful Thinking**

When I was a teenager, I was working on building my brother-in-law's home. He asked me to pour cement and rocks in the footings for the addition to the house. When the forms were removed, my terrible work was revealed. There were all sorts of air holes in the footings. I had not stuffed in the cement well enough. Had the footings been left that way, the building likely would collapse. In a perverted but similar way, pride is the faulty foundation for all the other kinds of evil thinking.

Hurtful thinking is, "I am better than he is (pride); I'll get him." Fearful thinking is, "What's going to happen to me (pride)." Lustful thinking is, "I want this for myself (pride)." Self pity says, "I don't deserve this (pride)."

Let's take a little closer look at this. Micah 2:1-3 reads:

"Woe to those who plan iniquity, to those who plot evil on their beds! At morning's light they carry it out because it is in their power to do it. They covet fields

and seize them, and houses, and take them. They
defraud a man of his home, a fellowman of his inheritance. Therefore, the Lord says: 'I am planning
disaster against this people, from which you cannot
save yourselves. You will no longer walk proudly, for it
will be a time of calamity.' "

Notice the planning, thinking activity that goes on at
night on their beds. They plan to lustfully grab things for
themselves. Verse 2 says they covet, and then describes
this in verse 3 as walking "proudly". So God points out
the foundational relationship of pride to lustful thinking.
Because we think so well of ourselves, we think we
deserve people and things and we want to draw them to
us.

David shows that hurtful thoughts come from a base of
pride:

"Proud men have hidden a snare for me; they have
spread out the cords of their net and have set traps for
me along my path." (Psalm 140:5)

It is clear that the proud men are planning to hurt
David. The setting of traps takes planning. The mind is
sinfully active.

Why do they do it? A proud man (I call them me-firsters)
will see almost anyone as a threat to his own well-being.
So he goes after one with a vengeance. A man I consider
to be one of the most prideful people I have ever met
attacked me personally. I couldn't understand the ferocity
of the attacks until later when I began to see the link
between pride and hurtful thinking.

Carole Mayhall writes in Words That Hurt.Words That
Heal:

"When I memorized Proverbs 13:10 the lessons
bombarded me. It says, 'Only by pride cometh

contention' (KJV). I thought, Wait a minute here! Can this possibly mean that whenever I feel contentious, upset, or angry, it is due to pride? That's hard to swallow. So I began to check all my angry feelings against this verse. Pride is an unduly high opinion of yourself; exaggerated self-esteem. It is putting yourself and what you are doing ahead of others and what they are doing.

When Lynn, age three, dragged in three friends with muddy feet over my freshly cleaned and waxed kitchen floor, I was annoyed with her. Why? She hadn't considered my hard work (pride of self). When Jack brought unexpected company home for dinner, I was indignant. Why? He hadn't considered the extra work it was for me."

At the base of all sinful thinking, not just hurtful thinking, is pride. Proud thinking also has some powerful consequences.

**An Out-Of-Focus Brain**

The first consequence of proud thinking is that one cannot see with clarity. Things get out of focus. Colossians 2:18 discloses the nature of this distortion:

"Do not let anyone who delights in false humility and the worship of angels disqualify you for the prize. Such a person goes into great detail about what he has seen, and his unspiritual mind puffs him up with idle notions."

Notice that his unspiritual mind "puffs him up." That is a graphic description of mental pride. It is unspiritual. This is not God-centered thinking, but me-centered thinking. This person is all blown up, filled with self. He looks like a blimp, and his advertisement is, "Me".

Also note that the verse shows the product of such thinking - idle notions. This mind is focused on self, but everything else is out of focus. The result is that it can't even see itself with the right perspective. It is like a golfer who, after hacking his way through 17 holes, hits a tee shot on the 18th hole that is long and straight. He thinks that that one shot represents his true golfing ability and the 17 holes of poor shots are a result of bad luck.

David points out in Psalm 36:1-4:

> "An oracle is within my heart concerning the sinfulness of the wicked; there is no fear of God before his eyes. For in his own eyes he flatters himself too much to detect or hate his sin. The words of his mouth are wicked and deceitful; he has ceased to be wise and to do good. Even on his bed he plots evil; he commits himself to a sinful course and does not reject what is wrong."

A couple of things just jump out from the verses. First, the wicked are proud. This is clearly the sense of verse 2, where "in his own eyes he flatters himself." Also we see that this wicked person is involved in evil thinking; he plots evil on his bed.

What is the result of this thinking? He flatters himself too much to detect or hate his sin (v.2). He commits himself to a sinful course and does not reject what is wrong (v.4). He has lost the ability to see his sin. He thinks he's always right.

A man once told me, "I have the gift of truth." I came to learn that he didn't mean discernment in the usual sense, but that he thought he was always right. That is distorted thinking par excellence!

## The Great Barrier Reef

Off the shore of northeast Australia is located the famous Great Barrier Reef. It becomes very difficult to approach the coast because this natural barrier blocks the way. This illustrates the second consequence of proud thinking. It becomes so great a barrier reef to a person that people can't approach him.

A survey was once taken of many of the thousands of teens who ran away from home to New York City. Why did they leave? One of the two most common reasons was that their father would never admit he was wrong. Pride acted as a blockade. The child felt like he couldn't really approach a person who wouldn't ever admit to being wrong, and there is little doubt the teen's own pride helped put him on the bus to New York. Actually pride is a repellent that drives people away from each other.

Jesus had no pride at all, so people felt very comfortable about approaching Him. He presented no barrier. Jesus provides us with an example. There was no pride in Him. Look at His birthplace - a smelly stable. His hometown? Nazareth (Can anything good come from there?) His name? Jesus. As one writer points out,

"If Jesus came today, His name might have been John or Bob or Jim. Were He here today, it is doubtful He would distance Himself with a lofty name like Reverend Holiness Angelic Divinity III. No, when God chose the name His Son would carry, He chose a human name.     He chose a name so typical that it would appear two or three times on any given class roll."

**The Pathway To Destruction**

Proud thinking is destructive.    It will destroy your
relationships with others.  Anthony Campolo says,

> "Many people who consider themselves Christians
> remain at odds with each other because their pride will
> not allow them to make the confessions necessary for
> reconciliation.   There is the father who in an angry
> tirade orders his son out of the house, and then
> anguishes over what he has done.  But pride prevents
> him from going to his son to say that he is sorry.
> There is the deacon who verbally attacks his pastor at
> a church meeting, and stomps out of the church in a
> huff.  He misses the fellowship of his former church
> friends, but will not confess his sin because he is
> afraid of losing face."

Proud thinking also destroys your work for the Lord.  I
remember hearing a brilliant young teacher.  His insight
was fresh.  He was clear and powerful.  His messages were
life-changing.    But as I spoke with him personally, it
seemed as if pride oozed out of his pores.  As good and
talented as he was, pride got in the way.  I had wanted to
use him on several occasions, but my desire to use him
ebbed when I saw the pride.  I think that pride can destroy
a ministry.  Oh, that ministry might appear successful,
but the real spiritual fruit is bruised.
    When I graduated from Bible College, I felt like I was
bursting upon the scene with clear and perfect (or as near
perfect as unperfect humans can have) insight.   I had
correct doctrine and correct methods.  In short, I felt like I
was God's gift to the world.  As a teacher told another
budding speaker, "You can't convince people that you're
wonderful and that Jesus is wonderful in the same
sermon." A ministry that is full of self is not full of God.  A

ministry that is not full of God to the extent that it lacks God's fullness is going to fail.

Psalm 9:1 is David's credo, "I will praise you, O Lord, with all my heart." I have a Samoyed dog named Shishka. I have never known a dog so eager to please, a dog with such wholehearted devotion. Every morning as I wake, there she is eagerly waiting to go with me for my morning paper. As we approach the car, she is running in tight little circles. She's so excited, she's out of breath and trembling with nervous energy. As Shishka is devoted to me, so we need to be wholeheartedly devoted to God. This is an absolute necessity for our thinking to be pure.

We've been identifying sinful areas of thinking. With what areas do you struggle? It would be well for you to know what you have to fight against as we move to the next phase.

# PART II

# TURNING IT AROUND

# CHAPTER 7

# REGULATING WORLDLY INPUT

"Do not conform any longer to the pattern of this world,
but be transformed by the renewing of your mind.
Then you will be able to test and approve what God's
will is - His good, pleasing, and perfect will."

ROMANS 12: 2

We have sloshed through the ugly swamps of sinful thoughts, and now we can begin the climb out into a healthier climate. We will soon see that there are two ways to describe our climb. *Regulating of worldly input* is discussed in this chapter and *changing our minds* is discussed in the next chapter.

Our cabin in the Catskills has no electricity, and we depend heavily upon propane. We have several 20-pound tanks of propane gas which we use for light, cooking and even refrigeration. A fairly expensive device called a regulator determines the correct gas flow. Similarly, a faucet regulates the water flow, the amount of water; and in a single faucet system, one faucet regulates the amount of hot water and cold water. We need to use a mental regulator to regulate what comes into our minds.

**Some Scripture On Worldly Influence**

The first Psalm is a contrast between the righteous and the wicked. The righteous person is described in terms of what he doesn't do:

> "Blessed is the man who does not walk in the counsel of the wicked or stand in the way of sinners or sit in the seat of mockers." (v. 1).

Because the worldly person has only a human perspective, he is unable to see God's way, and as a result his counsel is warped and perverted by his humanistic mind-set.

There was a time when I was involved in a fairly lucrative business. One day God figuratively tapped me on the shoulder, and, eventually, I told God I would do whatever He wanted. This led me back to school to train for the ministry, but I kept my business operating. When I told relatives and business associates where I was headed, they thought I must be out of my mind to leave all that money and security. Henry David Thoreau said,

"If a man does not keep pace with his companions perhaps it is because he hears a different drummer. Let him step to the music which he hears, however measured or far away."

We Christians walk to the beat of God's drum, which requires different cadence than the world's. That's why they can't really understand us.

Now, this is not to say that a lost person never has anything good to say. I am not claiming that the world can't teach us some good things. All people are made in the image of God, and although all of us have been scarred by the fall, a lost man can still speak some truth, be honest and do socially good things.

The movie Jaws taught me some good lessons in standing alone for good. The sheriff was virtually the only one in the town that saw the danger of the shark. The business interests and the mayor wanted the beaches open. The sheriff fought almost alone against selfish thinking. It was a good lesson for me because Christians often have to stand alone for good. So we must regulate the input we get from the world to be sure it squares with God's Word.

Another passage that speaks to this is I John 2:15-16,

"Do not love the world or anything in the world. If anyone loves the world, the love of the Father is not in him. For everything in the world - the cravings of sinful man, the lust of his eyes and the boasting of what he has and does - comes not from the Father but from the world."

Here God strongly warns about warming up to the world. To follow the unregulated advice and teaching of the world suggests that the love of the Father is not in us a sobering thought.

## Some Sources of Worldly Influence

The first source I want to mention is secular teaching in schools. When Sir Edmund Hillary completed his first climb of Mt. Everest, he was so grateful to the efforts of the Nepalese, especially his co-laborer, sherpa guide Tenzing Norgay that he asked the people, "What can I do for you?", "Give us schools", they responded. Since there were almost no Nepalese teachers, they brought in Hindu Indian teachers. The result was an eroding of the sherpa culture. The Buddhist beliefs were watered down; the number of monks decreased. A whole culture changed because the teachers, who had the children's attention for many hours a week, taught something other than their parents' beliefs.

When you look at the subjects taught in the schools, you encounter many courses that are taught from a non-Christian perspective. Biology is undergirded with evolutionary theory. History discussions leave out the considerable contributions of Christianity. In literature, there is often study of morally inappropriate material. The Social sciences often are taught from an unbiblical point of view, and sex education can be, and usually is, an abomination.

Now the subjects may be good, but the teaching of that good subject is sometimes from an un-Christian, religiously anti-biblical viewpoint which sometimes is

militantly pro-secular and humanistic. Sometimes a
Christian teacher tries to wedge his opinion into the
system. In any case, the material must be regulated by
the Christian student and parent.

A second source of worldly input is television. Some is
obvious. Enormously popular shows such as "Night
Court" and "Cheers" blatantly present a lifestyle counter
to the Bible. Sex outside of marriage is the norm. Soaps
broadcast an almost totally unbiblical and worldly view of
life.

But then some of it is not so obvious. Joanmarie Kalter
wrote in TV Guide,

> "The teens at the mall happily recite all the programs
> they watch - The Cosby Show, Growing Pains, Who's
> the Boss?, Mr. Belvedere, My Two Dads, Kate and Allie
> - all the many family shows." Indeed, the vast majority
> of TV viewing among children is of adult programs.
> And according to a study by the National Institute of
> Mental Health, adults and children alike use TV to
> learn how to handle their own family roles. What then
> do these programs present as a model of behavior?
> And are the messages of today's family shows different
> from what they once were?"

She answers what the teaching is as she continues:

> "In family sitcoms, a lot of the kids seem to be into
> themselves," says Dr. Alvin Poussaint, a psychiatrist
> and consultant to the Cosby Show. "Everybody is
> going in their own direction, doing their own thing.
> They flit in and flit out, giving their one-liners and dis-
> appearing...There's a lot of emphasis on individual
> success and individual problems. The message is to
> pull together as a family, but they don't behave that
> way." One family-show producer, who asked not to be
> named, says, "The message is go for yourself...self-

actualization is more important than family...It's the highest shining value to be all you can be," as the commercials say." So while family shows may explicitly invoke social togetherness, they implicitly promote social isolation."

Now this is far more subtle. It isn't as easy to pick up. When Tempestt Bledsoe's character on The Cosby Show says, "You can't control love," she is affirming worldly belief. The Bible, however, commands us to love. We are to love our enemies. That is a controlled love. Yes, you can control love. But, you see, the ideas are subtle; they sneak up on you. We have to regulate them.

The third source of worldly input is music. One songwriter, Ken Medema, once told me that a songwriter can take his talent and make any style of music say whatever he wants it to say. The message can be godly or ungodly. Sometimes the song you hum might have a very ungodly message. Peggy Mann said in a recent article,

"Some of today's rock music extols everything from rape, incest and homosexuality to sadomasochism and bestiality - in words too graphic to be printed here. Other lyrics glamorize drug and alcohol use, and glorify death and violent rebellion, ranging from hatred of parents and teachers to suicide - the ultimate act of violence to oneself. Teen Vision, Inc., a Carnegie, Pa. non-profit media, found obscene material prevalent in up to one-third of all current rock releases surveyed. Since studies show that the average teenager listens to rock music four hours a day, according to our research," says DeMoss, "about 60 percent of metal lyrics rely on destructive, depressing or degrading themes."

She goes on to say,

"There is, of course, no way to determine whether a suicide would have occurred in any case, but don't tell that to the parents of 19-year-old John McCollum from Indio, California. When he killed himself, the coroner's report stated, "Decedent committed suicide by shooting self in head with .22 caliber pistol while listening to devil music." John, who had been getting an earful of Ozzy Osbourne albums for five hours, was wearing stereo headphones at the time of his death. He was hearing such messages as, "Suicide is the only way out" from "Suicide Solution" and "Can you help me? Oh, shoot out my brains, ohhh yeah...I tell you to end your life" from "Paranoid."

I've got to think that there's a correlation between the skyrocketing suicide rates among kids and the lyrics of the music they listen to. But now the question I want to pose is, "What do we do about it?"

## Regulate It

The Christian who just lets all this stuff flow freely into his cranium will inevitably accept more than he should. We should stand with our fingers on the faucet and our minds turned on full.

Sometimes to regulate properly you turn the faucet off. There are times I just turn a T.V. show off. As a family, we elected to turn off the valve of the public schools. We felt that the 40 hours or so of secular instruction was too much. That may not be for you, but we were absolutely certain Christian Schools were right for us.

Sometimes you regulate by letting some water go through but you monitor it closely. Lois Draper, a pastor's wife, titled an article, "Talk back to your TV set." What a great idea! We've used her concepts to have family discussions about philosophies that have come out of our

TV set. When commercials promote materialism, we talk back. It's been a very healthy way for us to deal with the problems. Why don't you take some paper and write down a list of all the things that go against Scripture that you see on T.V. for one week. It might be an eye-opening experience for you.

Regulating may mean turning the valve off, or letting some in by carefully checking it with the Bible, but it is a necessary exercise in the arena of the mind.

# CHAPTER 8

# changing our minds

"Therefore, I urge you brothers, in view of God's mercy,
to offer your bodies as living sacrifices, holy and pleasing
to God - this is your spiritual act of worship. Do not
conform any longer to the pattern of this world, but be
transformed by the renewing of your mind. Then you
will be able to test and approve what God's will is - his
good, pleasing and perfect will."

ROMANS 12: 1,2

They say that it's a woman's prerogative to change her mind. Usually that means a change of opinion, or a new decision. God's desire for us is transformation -- a complete and *radical* change of mind.

Carole Mayhall says,

> "Many people in our society today wrestle with unbelievable difficulties that cling to their lives like blood suckers. They have been victims of emotional or physical abuse, had marriages full of pain and anger, and have been violated, humiliated, and torn apart inside.
>
> How they respond to these hurts varies greatly. Some are able, with the help of Christ, to forget those things that are behind them. (Philippians 3:13). Others seem unable or unwilling to let the hurts go. They continually relive the ugly situations over and over in their minds. Consequently, they do not think about 'whatever is lovely'. (Philippians 4:8). They keep reloading into their minds thoughts from a tragic past, and live in depression and despair as they are haunted by those thoughts."

Why is it that some break through all the garbage and others mentally wallow in it? We come now to the pivotal point. We are going to talk about how you can change your thinking from sinful to godly patterns. Regulating your thinking by limiting the worldly input is almost like preventative maintenance. It is important. Anyone familiar with computers knows "garbage in, garbage out" means that if the material programmed into the computer is garbage, the computer will spit out garbage. This is

also true of thought patterns. Now, however, we move to
the actual process of changing habitual thought patterns
already in place.


## Repentance - Biblical Style

When we talk about change the operative biblical word
is repentance. It is a word that is out of vogue as John
MacArthur points out so well in The Gospel According to
Jesus, but it is a word that is often repeated in the Bible.

Jesus used it early in His ministry, "From that time on
Jesus began to preach, 'Repent, for the kingdom of heaven
is near.'" (Matthew 4:17) He made it clear that repentance
is what we need.      Repentance is also urged in
Luke 13:1-5:

> "Now there were some present at that time who told
> Jesus about the Galileans whose blood Pilate had
> mixed with their sacrifices. Jesus answered, "Do you
> think that these Galileans were worse sinners than all
> the other Galileans because they suffered this way? I
> tell you, no!  But unless you repent, you too will all
> perish.  Or those eighteen who died when the tower in
> Siloam fell on them - do you think they were more
> guilty than all the others living in Jerusalem?  I tell
> you, no!  But unless you repent, you too will all
> perish."

Repentance is necessary to avoid eternal destruction.
In commanding His disciples after His resurrection about
what to do from then on Jesus says:

> "He told them, 'This is what is written: The Christ
> will suffer and rise from the dead on the third day, and
> repentance and forgiveness of sins will be preached in

his name to all nations, beginning at Jerusalem.' " (Luke 24:46-47).

So Jesus's message is full of our need to repent. But what does it mean to repent?

The Greek word is METANOIA which is made up of two words, META 'after' and NOUS 'mind'. The combined idea is a mind change. Thayer's Lexicon of the Greek New Testament defines it this way: "Used especially of those who, conscious of their sins and with manifest tokens of sorrow, are intent on obtaining God's pardon.

To change one's mind for the better, heartily amend or abhorrence of one's past sins."

Some years ago, my niece, Kathy, married and moved to California. While there, they got hold of a pet - a tawny, cute, lovable lion cub. Lion cubs, however, don't stay small long. When this one had grown to about 200 pounds, they decided to move East. When they knocked on my sister's door, they were told, "You can come in, but the lion stays out." So they left the lion in the car! Now, use your imagination. What do you think the insides of that car looked like? (Never mind what it smelled like)! Obviously, the situation was intolerable. Obviously, they had to find a more suitable place for their lion to live.

An adventurous farmer in the northwestern corner of New Jersey said he would like to take the lion. After lengthy instruction on lion care and feeding, the farmer took possession of one 200-pound, male lion. Well, it's one thing to want a pet like that and quite another to have it. He put the cat in the living room and closed the door. Now put yourself in his shoes. Once that door was closed, would you open it? Well, he didn't. The living room quickly became a den - a lion's den. He watched through the window in horror as a one-cat wrecking crew systematically destroyed everything in the room. You see, he was told he had to play with the lion. He didn't. So the lion found things to play with - like sofas and chairs, which he merrily batted around. So Tom and Kathy were called to rescue the farmer.

This is where I come into the story. We lived in the country and had a very sturdy dog pen; so I called Tom and said, "You can keep the lion at our place." I made it clear he was to do the feeding; after all, those things eat a lot of food.

The next thing you know, Tom and Kathy arrived with the lion. They drove an 8-foot stake into the ground and chained him to it. He climbed up on the roof of the dog house and draped one huge paw over the edge striking a regal pose - king of all he surveyed.

Now we had a husky named Rocks who knew something unusual was going on. His ears were alert, his tail was curled over his back. I guess his nose told him there was a cat outside on his turf, and he barked aggressively to let the intruder know he was coming. When we let Rocks out, he charged the pen barking furiously, ears and tail held high. But when he was about twenty feet from the pen, the lion ROARED. Rocks REPENTED!! His ears went flat. The tail uncurled and went under his body so fast that he smacked himself in the chops. The aggressive bark became whimpering and squealing. He did a 180 degree U-turn and sprinted for his life out the driveway and into the woods.

The roar of the lion caused him to voluntarily and radically change. His attitude, bearing, and behavior all were different. True repentance is a significant change of mind.

## Elements of Repentance

There are three elements in repentance: Sorrow, choice, and change. Let's look at each one. Sorrow is first.

In an article on how to conquer addictions, Norma Petersen says that Stage 1 is accumulated unhappiness about the addiction. She quotes Dr. Stanton Peele, a psychologist with the Human Resources Institutes of Morristown, N.J., "You have to believe the rewards you'll get (from quitting) will surpass what you get from the habit." She goes on:

"Cynthia Morgan of Santa Cruz, Calif., says she thought about quitting smoking for years but decided to do it when she turned 35 and realized that smoking was affecting not just her health but also her looks."

But the Bible shows that repentance involves greater sorrow. When I realize that I have sinned against a holy God, and I see the enormity of it, I cry out with David,

"Have mercy on me, O God. according to your unfailing love; according to your great compassion, blot out my transgressions. Wash away all my iniquity and cleanse me from my sin.

For I know my transgressions, and my sin is always before me.

Against you, you only, have I sinned and done what is evil in your sight. so that you are proved right when you speak and justified when you judge.

Surely I was sinful at birth, sinful from the time my mother conceived me.

Surely you desire truth in the inner parts; you teach me wisdom in the inmost place.

Cleanse me with hyssop, and I will be clean; wash me, and I will be whiter than snow.

Let me hear joy and gladness; let the bones you have crushed rejoice.

Hide your face from my sins and blot out all my iniquity.

Create in me a pure heart, O God, and renew a steadfast spirit within me." (Psalm 51:1-10)

That's the sorrow of repentance!

Second, repentance involves choice. It is a choice to change your mind. Edmund Haggai says,

> "The majority of people who are chronic worriers make the ridiculous mistake of waiting until the circumstances engulfing them change. You must change the circumstances whenever possible."

Norma Petersen's second stage is called "a moment of truth." She states:

> "Most ex-addicts can pinpoint a moment at which they became disgusted, and that moment hatched their escape. Peele says, 'For Darlene Mahan of Andover, Mass., the moment of truth came the day she got onto a roller coaster and the protective bar wouldn't close over her girth. In the next two years she lost 173 pounds.' "

The "moment of truth" is when a choice is made - a choice to stop doing one thing and start doing another. Jesus made this choice very clear in Luke 14:25-33,

> "Large crowds were traveling with Jesus, and turning to them he said: If anyone comes to me and does not hate his father and mother, his wife and children, his brothers and sisters yes, even his own life - he cannot be my disciple. And anyone who does not carry his cross and follow me cannot be my disciple.
>
> Suppose one of you wants to build a tower. Will he not first sit down and estimate the cost to see if he has enough money to complete it? For if he lays the foundation and is not able to finish it, everyone who sees it will ridicule him, saying, this fellow began to build and was not able to finish.

Or suppose a king is about to go to war against another king. Will he not first sit down and consider whether he is able with ten thousand men to oppose the one coming against him with twenty thousand. If he is not able, he will send a delegation while the other is still a long way off and will ask for terms of peace. In the same way, any of you who does not give up everything he has cannot be my disciple."

Counting the cost is going over your options. I can choose to go on living as I am, or I can choose to live as Christ commands. But there's a huge cost, and I need to consider that.

The third thing is change. Romans 12:2 says,

"Do not conform any longer to the pattern of this world, but be transformed by the renewing of your mind. Then you will be able to test and approve what God's will is - his good, pleasing and perfect will."

Here is radical change! Transformation and renewal of my mind means a basic difference. When I was young, my parents didn't want a dog but they allowed me to have a cat. So one day I proudly brought home a slate-gray kitten. There was a family that lived in our neighborhood during the summer. They had a Welsh Terrier that became a terror to my little kitten. This terrier-fied kitten would be chased almost daily up into the sanctuary of a tree. Mercifully, the family went away after Labor Day.

During the Fall and Winter, the kitten grew into a cat and it befriended a golden retriever. On one occasion, I saw the dog running with the cat on his back. They romped together into the late Spring. Then one day the neighbors returned for their summer stay. I know that dogs have memory because when their terrier got out of the car, he smiled. He remembered all the fun of the chase and bounded joyfully off towards our house, saw the cat, and launched his charge. But something was wrong. The cat wasn't running. It was, in fact, arched. Have you ever seen an arched cat? They look like MacDonalds arches. All their fur stands out, looking for all the world like a porcupine. They look all brittle; like they would break if you touched them. She hissed viciously. The dog put on the brakes, and they faced off about six feet apart.

I don't know how she did it in that arched position, but she took a step toward the dog. Then she walked up to him and flashed a paw full of extended claws. Whap! She nailed him right on the nose. Now the dog executed an incredible maneuver. He jumped straight up and turned 180 degrees and fled for his life. But the thing that really amazed me was the cat chased him all the way home! This was a changed cat!

Paul said,

"First to those in Damascus, then to those in Jerusalem and in all Judea, and to the Gentiles also, I preached that they should repent and turn to God and prove their repentance by their deeds." (Acts 26:20).

Deeds prove one's repentance. They show change.

Now we need to look at this act of repentance in two ways. First, repentance is a voluntary act on our part at the time we are saved. It is in this way a once-and-done, cataclysmic act. But there is a second way. Once I have repented and am a born-again, saved person, as God's Spirit makes me aware of them, I still need to repent of sins. John makes this clear,

"If we claim to be without sin, we deceive ourselves and the truth is not in us. If we confess our sins, he is faithful and just and will forgive us our sins and purify us from all unrighteousness. If we claim we have not sinned, we make him out to be a liar and his word has no place in our lives." I John 1:8-10.

Verses 8 and 10 show me that the Christian is aware of sin. He sees it clearly. He mourns over it (Matthew 5:3). But confession of specific sins brings forgiveness and cleansing.

Albert N. Martin illustrated it this way. He said it was like the Pacific theater of World War II and especially, to the battle for Iwo Jima. The huge guns of the U.S. naval vessels pounded that island for hours so that one would wonder how anything could still be alive. But when the Marines hit the beaches, they knew that many were not only alive, but fighting fiercely. The plan was to take Mt. Suribachi, and the Marines slowly won their way up the flanks of that blood-stained mountain. Finally, the climactic moment came when the four Marines lifted our flag at the top. The island was won! Or was it? It's true that the U.S. controlled the island, but there were still many of the Japanese Army hidden away in caves, and the mopping up that went on, sometimes for years, was a nasty, deadly business.

There is a repentance that is like the taking of Mt. Suribachi. It is the climactic moment when I surrender to Jesus Christ as Lord, trust Him as Savior. At that moment the flag that flies over me is His flag. He controls me, but hiding in the caves of my being, especially in the deep recesses of my mind, there are still nests of sin that must be slowly, painfully dug out. This work involves repentance too, and it is the work of a lifetime. This second kind of repentance involves our thinking.

**Putting Off Sinful Thinking**

Two passages set the pattern for dealing with sin.
The first is Ephesians 4:22-24 which says,

"You were taught, with regard to your former way of life, to put off your old self, which is being corrupted by its deceitful desires; to be made new in the attitude of your minds; and to put on the new self, created to be like God in true righteousness and holiness."

Simply said, it is to put off the old self and the old patterns of thought - all the sinful areas of thinking we identified such as self pity, fearful, hurtful, lustful and proud thoughts. Then, with a changed attitude of mind, we must put on a new self with new thought patterns.

A second passage is Colossians 3:1-5:

"Since, then , you have been raised with Christ, set your hearts on things above, where Christ is seated at the right hand of God. Set your minds on things above, not on earthly things. For you died, and your life is now hidden with Christ in God. When Christ, who is your life, appears, then you also will appear with Him in glory. Put to death, therefore, whatever belongs to your earthly nature; sexual immorality, impurity, lust, evil desires, and greed, which is idolatry."

Then verse 12 adds:

"Therefore, as God's chosen people, holy and dearly loved, clothe yourselves with compassion, kindness, humility, gentleness and patience."

Again, the thinking process is very important. We are to set our minds on things above,  to put to death things of the old nature and to clothe ourselves in godly characteristics.

The process is putting off and putting on -- putting off sinful thoughts, and putting on righteous thoughts.

There are two things I can suggest to help to put off sinful thoughts. The first has to do with getting rid of mental triggers. You mention something to a friend, and he says, "Don't get me started..." What happened? What you said triggered a mental process that he realized was bad and so he tried to stop it. Triggers set off sinful thinking. Lustful thoughts, for example, can be triggered by all sorts of things.

Obviously a picture of a naked, seductively posed woman would get mental wheels of lust turning, but so can almost any woman if we allow ourselves to gaze. One friend of mine calls it "the turning of the head." This is what Job meant when he said, "I made a covenant with my eyes not to look lustfully at a girl" (Job 31:1). He determined to eliminate the second look. He would get rid of that trigger.

At this point, let me ask you, "What triggers your sinful thoughts?" It is important to identify what sets you off. After you have identified areas of sinful thinking with which you struggle, take each one and determine what things set you off. These are the triggers. Romans 12:14b (NASB) commands, "Make no provision for the flesh." When you identify the triggers, purpose to eliminate them.

A counselor was trying to help a man conquer lustful thoughts. Finally, he found that the man habitually walked by an "adult" theater. As he gazed on the pictures, he was inexorably drawn into lustful thinking. The theater was a trigger. He didn't have to walk down that street. Going a different way removed the trigger.

The second method of eliminating sinful thoughts is prayer. Maybe your experience is like mine. All too often in the midst of a temptation I cry out "Help me," and nothing happens. Maybe it's because I don't really want help, but whatever the reason, too often my prayer for help has been ineffective.

One thing I've learned that has been very helpful, is that when I am in the midst of temptation or I can see it coming, I pray "theologically." I ask my Father to help me on the basis of the blood of Christ. I can refer to that incredibly costly act of love that paid for this sin. I can ask for the temptation to be removed because Jesus' blood paid for my sin. Paul makes this claim:

> "No temptation has seized you except what is common to man. And God is faithful; He will not let you be tempted beyond what you can bear. But when you are tempted He will also provide a way out so that you can stand up under it (I Corinthians 10:13)."

There are tremendous promises here. We can stand up under any temptation. We have the resources available. Whenever I pray, as I have outlined above, referring to the blood of Christ, the temptation has dissolved. I say to my own shame I don't always do it, but when I have, God has given me the way out, and I have withstood.

But now I must bring up a problem. Jesus told us,

> "When an evil spirit comes out of a man, it goes through arid places seeking rest and does not find it. Then it says, 'I will return to the house I left. When it arrives, it finds the house unoccupied, swept clean and put in order. Then it goes and takes with it seven other spirits more wicked than itself, and they go in and live there. And the final condition of that man is worse than the first. That is how it will be with this wicked generation.' " (Matthew 12:43-45).

This teaches us that we have to do more than empty out the bad thoughts. We must not be spiritual "airheads." Temptation will return worse than ever if the house is swept clean and empty. No, we have to fill it, fill it with godly thoughts. Then temptation is more easily warded off.

This then will be our focus for the rest of the book - filling our minds with Godly thoughts.

# PART III

# TRANSFORMING OUR MINDS

# CHAPTER 9

# The Truth Hurts...
# Evil Thoughts

"In my own little corner, in my own little chair,
  I can be whatever I want to be
      On the wings of my fancy, I can go anywhere
      And the world opens it's arms to me."

RICHARD ROGERS AND OSCAR HAMMERSTEIN'S
MUSICAL CINDERELLA

When Jeremiah was a young man, the Bible records God's Word coming to him:

"Before I formed you in the womb, I knew you, before you were born I set you apart; I appointed you as a prophet to the nations." (Jeremiah 1:5).

In the tradition of Moses, Jeremiah's fertile mind came up with an excuse - too young. God's answer in effect was "You're simply going to have to do it." Then He outlined what the ministry would be:

"Then the Lord reached out His hand and touched my mouth and said to me, 'Now, I have put my words in your mouth. See, today I appoint you over nations and kingdoms to uproot and tear down, to destroy and overthrow, to build and to plant.' " (Jeremiah 1:9-10).

This ministry of Jeremiah's was to have two thrusts. After tearing down evil, he would build and plant. We have seen this in the arena of the mind. The established thoughts must be uprooted. Only then can the seeds of godly thoughts be planted.

Jesus used an illustration of four kinds of soil that receive the seed of God's word. One kind of soil is called the thorny ground. The farmer had no doubt burned off his field, and the good seeds landed on soil that had the established root systems of thorny thistles that are really the size of large bushes. When the seed started to sprout, these fast growing thorns crowd it out so that the seed produces a shriveled, fruitless, and therefore useless plant.

Similarly, we must first uproot the evil thought patterns before attempting to establish godly ones. But, as we have seen, when the evil thoughts have been expunged, unless we replace them, they'll come back again like an unwanted cat.

So then, we come to the place in our journey where we must talk about filling our minds with godly thoughts. Philippians 4:8 is the key verse for this whole section. It says:

"Finally, brothers, whatever is true, whatever is noble, whatever is right, whatever is pure, whatever is lovely, whatever is admirable - if anything is excellent or praise worthy - think about such things."

Godly thinking is summarized in eight words which are the subject of the next eight chapters. We'll seek to describe what kind of thinking is meant and how to use each kind of thinking to replace a particular kind of evil thinking.

**True Thinking - What It Is**

The first word in the list is true. The Greek word is ALETHEIA, and there are two concepts that are derived from this word:

- Meaning #1 -        *Whatever is real as opposed to whatever is fake.*

- Meaning #2 -        *Whatever is true as opposed to whatever is false.*

**What Is Real As Opposed To What Is Fake**

Much unreal thinking is fantasy. In Rodgers &
Hammerstein's musical, "Cinderella," Leslie Ann Warren
sang a touching song. Cinderella was left at home,
splotched with dust, while her evil sisters were out
attempting to find the good life. The song went, in part,

"In my own little corner, in my own little chair, I can
be whatever I want to be. On the wings of my fancy, I
can go anywhere, and the world opens its arms to me."

Les Paul and Mary Ford many years ago sang, "Just
wrap your troubles in dreams, and dream your troubles
away." More recently, Dr. Ruth has been touting the
virtues of fantasy in sexuality.

Hardly any godly person would advise others to escape
trouble by downing a fifth of bourbon. He knows that
when the bag of warm stupor is unzipped, one crawls out
into a cold, clear world of reality. The facts come crashing
down, and he hasn't escaped at all, only postponed.

Fantasy of every sort comes in all shapes and sizes from
sexual fantasy and the TV-induced fantasy of soaps to the
wonderful world of worry. If ever there was an area of
unreal thinking, worry is it.

Remember this sequence...

My son is late - fact.

Maybe he had an accident - fantasy (complete with
mental pictures of ambulances, hospitals, doctors and
huge debts.)

Maybe he will be paralyzed - fantasy (accompanied by
questions: How will I take care of him? How will I pay
for it? etc. etc.)

**Mental Help For Worry-Warts**

Since true thinking is in part thinking in realistic terms,
real thinking is a replacement for all kinds of fantasy, but
as an example, let's apply it to worry.

Facing reality really helps the veteran worrier in three
ways.

First, he can realize what reality is.  W. Philip Keller in
Taming Tensions, claims that 80% of our fears never
materialize.  He goes on:

> "This figure of 80 percent is not guesswork.  It has
> been arrived at through extensive research.  And those
> of us who have lived long enough to look back on a
> good span of life know it to be true.  There are so many
> extenuating, changing, unpredictable, and unknown
> circumstances at play in life that in many cases, by the
> time a crisis has been reached, it is no longer a crisis.
> Circumstances change; people change; other events
> enter the scene; and we ourselves alter our minds so
> much that often what looms as a calamity in due
> course levels out to be but a minor matter.  What we
> imagined was an unclimbable mountain is stepped
> over like a small molehill."

This isn't going to do it all by itself, but it should help
you to realize that most of our fears don't come true.

By the way, reality could break up a self-pity party.  An
honest evaluation of what my situation is, what others
have done and what God has done goes a long way toward
replacing thoughts of self-pity.

The second way real thoughts can replace worry is by
concentration on "today" rather than "tomorrow".  Jesus
exclaimed,

"Therefore do not worry about tomorrow, for tomorrow will worry about itself. Each day has enough trouble of its own." (Matthew 6:34).

The key to understanding this passage lies in the word "tomorrow". What does it mean? James 4:13-16 brings the meaning to light:

"Now listen, you who say, 'Today or tomorrow we will go to this or that city, spend a year there, carry on business and make money.' Why you do not even know what will happen tomorrow. What is your life? You are a mist that appears for a little while and then vanishes. Instead, you ought to say, 'If it is the Lord's will, we will live and do this or that.' As it is, you boast and brag. All such boasting is evil."

We don't know what will happen tomorrow. "Tomorrow" embodies all that I can't control.

I can't control whether it will rain or not. I can't control economic conditions. I can't control how people respond to me. I can control how I respond, but I have no control over how others react.

The solution is found in thinking and acting in the realm of "today." Today comprises all the things I can control. I can control my own attitude. I can control my preparation so that if it does rain, I can be ready. So, again, real thinking involves planning. It deals with contingencies.

Thirdly, realistic true thinking smashes worry right in the breadbasket. We can be realistic about commitments.

We live in a crazy, frantic world. There is just so much to do. The tendency is to be over-committed. Too many things are vying for our time. Worriers are devastated by these circumstances because they wonder, "Will I be able to do it?" or "What should I do first?" Sometimes indecision's grip becomes so strong that paralysis results.

Worry sees an impenetrable forest, but realism sees one tree that can be cut down and then another and one more, until there is a pathway through the once impenetrable forest.  Realistic thinking looks at what I can actually do, lays out a plan to accomplish it, and rolls up its sleeves and gets to work.  Such thinking short-circuits worry.

Let's move on to the next building block in our house of good thinking.

# CHAPTER 10

# Non-Trivial Pursuit

YESTERDAY IS A CANCELLED CHECK.

TOMORROW IS A PROMISSORY NOTE.

TODAY IS THE ONLY CASH YOU HAVE -

SPEND IT WISELY.
                                    DR. PAUL LEE TAN

A few years back when Jack Nicklaus was the best golfer in the world, he played an exhibition in Reading, Pennsylvania where I was ministering. Several thousand avid golf fans paid handsomely to watch Jack play a then up-and-coming amateur, Betsy King. As we followed them around the course, I was impressed by two things: Jack Nicklaus had incredible skill as a golfer, and he was also a cheerful, genuinely nice person. As he was putting on the eighteenth green, I was suddenly struck with a thought: One day Jack Nicklaus will stand before God. God would ask, "Jack, what did you do on earth?" Jack would reply," I was the very best person in the world at putting a golf ball in a hole." Wow! I could see how we idolize athletes and entertainment personalities, and yet what they do in God's scheme of things is relatively trivial. We often pay much heed to the pursuit of trivia.

The second word in the profile of godly thinking in Philippians 4:8 is noble. The Greek word, SEMNA means that which inspires awe, majesty, seriousness. I would sum up its meaning by the word *important*. It is the opposite of trivial.


**The Pursuit of Non-Trivial Concept #1:**
**Preciousness to God**

The first of two ideas that have helped me to concentrate on important things is the concept of preciousness to God. In men's Bible study, one man mentioned something that he thought was precious to God. That clicked in my mind. "What could be more important for me to think about than whatever is precious to God." This helped me make sure I mentally focused on important things rather than frittering away my time on trivia.

A trip to the Concordance reveals several things that are precious to God. One of them is found in Psalm 48:7,8:

> "No man can redeem the life of another or give to God a ransom for him - the ransom for a life is costly, no payment is ever enough."

Life is precious to God. This opens up a host of areas of important thinking for me. As one who is in the pro-life movement, there are many projects and activities that I can plan and consider, and all of which are aimed at saving lives, and consequently are precious to God.

God's word reveals many things that are precious to God as well. But in addition, as we get to know God's character and attributes, we can begin to figure out for ourselves what is precious to Him. This, then, is a way to keep our thinking on track.

### The Pursuit of Non-Trivial Concept #2: Building Memorials

A second concept that helps me keep my thinking on important things is the practice that pops up from time to time in the Bible - building memorials. One such incident occurs in Joshua 4:1-7:

> "When the whole nation had finished crossing the Jordan, the Lord said to Joshua, 'Choose twelve men from among the people, one from each tribe, and tell them to take up twelve stones from the middle of the Jordan from right where the priests stood and to carry them over with you and put them down at the place where you stay tonight.'

"So Joshua called together the twelve men he had appointed from the Israelites, one from each tribe, and said to them, 'Go over before the ark of the Lord your God into the middle of the Jordan. Each of you is to take up a stone on his shoulder, according to the number of the tribes of the Israelites, to serve as a sign among you. In the future, when your children ask you, 'What do these stones mean?' Tell them that the flow of the Jordan was cut off before the ark of the covenant of the Lord. When it crossed the Jordan, the waters of the Jordan were cut off. These stones are to be a memorial to the people of Israel forever.' "

The pile of stones was to remind them of that event. The building of memorials is a helpful thing; but I'm thinking of it more as the building of good memories.

Charles Swindoll tells a story in <u>Seasons of Life</u> that illustrates the building of memories:

" 'You guys go on without me. You'll have a great time - I'm sure of that. Sorry, family, I have to work.'

| | |
|---|---|
| The place: | Montgomery, Alabama. |
| The time: | Several years ago. |
| The situation: | A dad, who really loved his family and wanted them to enjoy a summer vacation, had to work. The press of business kept him tied to the office. But being committed to their happiness, he assured them of his desire, that they take the trip and enjoy the fleeting summer days. |

He helped them plan every day of the camping trip. They would load up the family station wagon, drive to California, camp up and down the coast, then travel back home together. Each day was carefully arranged - even the highways they would travel and the places they would stop. Dad knew their whole route, the time they would reach each state - planned almost to the hour - even when they would cross the Great Divide.

It's what he didn't tell them that made the difference.

The father took off work (he'd planned it all along) and arranged to have himself flown to an airport near where his family would be on the particular day of the trip. He had also arranged to have someone pick him up and drive him to a place where every car on that route had to pass. With a wide grin, he sat on his sleeping bag and waited for the arrival of that familiar station wagon packed full of kids and camping gear. When he spotted the station wagon, he stood up, stepped out onto the shoulder of the road, and stuck out his thumb.

Can you visualize it?

'Look! That guy looks just like... DAD!'

The family assumed he was a thousand miles away, sweating over a stack of papers. It's amazing they didn't drive off into a ditch or collapse from heart failure. Can you imagine the fun they had the rest of the way? And the memories they stored away in their mental scrapbook - could they ever be forgotten?

When later asked why he would go to all that trouble, the creative father replied, 'Well, someday I'm going to be dead. When that happens, I want my kids and wife to say, 'You know, Dad was a lot of fun.' ".

Here was a man that did a whole lot of planning and scheming to pull off something that his family will always remember. We spend vast amounts of time on trivia - on things that won't matter a few years from now and on things that will pale in significance when we stand before God. Let's focus on what is really important.

## This Warns us NOT To Think So Much About Trivial Things

A booklet whose impact to me far outweighed its tiny size is Tyranny Of The Urgent by Charles E. Hummel. One passage reads,

"Several years ago an experienced cottonmill manager said to me, 'Your greatest danger is letting the urgent things crowd out the important.' He didn't realize how hard his maxim hit. It often returns to haunt and rebuke me by raising the critical problem of priorities."

All too frequently, a couple sits across from me pouring out how their marriage is coming apart. The frayed threads that hold it together are at the breaking point. Soon the problems emerge and they are sent away armed with assignments designed to deal with those problems.

Many return a week later with the assignments done. They realized the importance of working to save and revitalize their marriage, and they went to work on those problems and they are seeing progress.

Sadly, some return with the assignments not done. Oh, yes, there were all sorts of things that came up. Sure, they were urgent. But were they more important? Usually not! So often the disaster of divorce is hastened by the crowding out of the important by the urgent.

All too often we are possessed by what is urgent to the exclusion of what is important. We need to jump off that merry-go-round, and stop and think, "What is important?" Then we need to do those things.

**This Encourages Us To Think About Important Things**

On a warm spring day, I sat on the deck of our cabin in a white pine and hemlock glen. I had given myself two days of uninterrupted time to spend writing out my values. I had been challenged to do this while listening to tapes of a time management seminar. So I pulled up a lounge chair, and as the warm sunbeams filtered through the towering evergreens and the stream beside the cabin babbled its song, I worked over several pages that described what is important to me. These were already there in my mind, but I brought them out and wrote them down. During those two wonderful days, I developed these values regarding my relationship with God:

VALUE #1     I need to constantly express to God His infinite worth.
             I do this by:

*(To Him)*
- Telling Him how I know He is God.
- Telling Him what characteristics I like about Him.
- Telling Him what He has made that I like.
- Telling Him what He has done that I like.
- Expressing gratitude to Him.
*(To Others)*
- Expressing my gratitude about Him to others.
- Telling others what He has made and done that I like.
- Telling others what characteristics I like about Him.
- Telling others how I know He is God.
- Giving Him the credit that is due Him, and not taking it myself.
- Not being ashamed of Him.

VALUE #2    I need to constantly work to improve my
            relationship with Him.
            I do this by:

    •   Trying to learn His ways from His Word.
    •   Understanding His will by assimilating His
        Word.
    •   Communicating with Him in prayer.
    •   Being with people who are walking with
        Him.

VALUE #3    I need to constantly strive to be like Jesus.
            I do this by:

    •   Seeking to develop the Christ-like qualities
        found in His Word.
    •   Following the example of Christ as recorded
        in Scripture.

VALUE #4    I need to constantly serve others.
            I do this by:

    •   Learning, using, and sharpening my gifts,
        talents and abilities God has given to me, to
        help others.
    •   Being a good example.
    •   Seeking to prioritize the events of my life
        according to godly patterns.

This is only an example of what is important to me. Of
course, my relationship to God is the most important, but
other values are important too:   family, church, and
vocation.  These also should be worked out.  I heartily
recommend the writing out of one's general values as a
starting point in developing noble thinking.
    A second phase in developing what is really important is
to take time at the beginning of each month to set out

what you want to accomplish. One way of doing this is to
set goals in personal areas. Goals can be set for daily
devotions, for example. Here are some possibilities:

- Scheduling to read through the Bible in a year.
  Memorizing a passage (ie., the Sermon on the
  Mount: Matthew 5,6 and 7).
- Memorizing a book.
- Studying a half hour a day for a certain number of
  days per month.
- Reading the passages and notes from a study Bible
  for a half hour per day as above.

It is also good to set goals regarding personal habits. I
am involved in my own personal "Battle of the Bulge".
Each month I aim for a certain weight. I plan a number of
times of exercise each week. All the habits I want to
eliminate and good habits to be built can be goals for the
month. These goals can be written down before the
month begins and checked out periodically as the month
develops.

A third phase of fostering important thoughts is a daily
planning time. A challenge thrown out by Hyrum Smith of
The Franklin Institute is to take ten minutes a day every
day to spend in planning and solitude so that you can
determine what your day ought to be like.

Kent Hughes recounts this conversation in Liberating
Ministry From The Success Syndrome,

"A number of years ago a fascinating interview took
place between Mr. Charles Schwab, then president of
Bethlehem Steel, and Ivy Lee, a self-styled
management consultant. Lee was an aggressive, self-
confident man who by his perseverance had secured
the interview with Mr. Schwab, who was no less self-
assured, being one of the most powerful men in the
world. During the conversation, Mr. Lee asserted that

if the management of Bethlehem Steel would follow his advice, the company's operations would be improved and their profits increased.

Schwab responded, 'If you can show us a way to get more things done, I'll be glad to listen; and if it works, I'll pay you whatever you ask within reason.'

Lee handed Schwab a blank pieceof paper and said, 'Write down the most important things you have to do tomorrow.'

Mr. Schwab did so.

'Now,' Lee continued, 'number them in order of importance.'

Mr. Schwab did so.

'Tomorrow morning start on number one, and stay with it until you have completed it. Then go on to number two and number three and number four...Don't worry if you haven't completed everything by the end of the day. At least you have completed the most important projects. Do this every day. After you have been convinced of the value of this system, have your men try it. Try it as long as you like, and then send me your check for whatever you think the advice is worth.'

The two men shook hands and Lee left the president's office. A few weeks later, Charles Schwab sent Ivy Lee a check for $25,000 - an astronomical amount in the 1930's! He said it was the most profitable lesson he had learned in his long business career."

This is important thinking. If we do this daily and monthly and if we decide on what is really important in our lives, then it is far more likely that we won't be so involved in trivial pursuit.

# CHAPTER 11

# *And Justice For All*

that's
not fair

– any child of
any age
at almost any time.

"That's not fair!". Anyone who is a parent has heard these words of accusation as they countlessly pour from the lips of their children. "I was here first." "She got more." "How come I can't, and he can?" Whereupon the parent patiently, and sometimes not so patiently, attempts to explain why it is fair after all.

The next word in our list of proper thinking from Philippians 4:8 is "right." This is translated from the Greek word DIKAIOS. It means upright, just, fair, not prejudiced. So when the child cries, "Not fair," the claim is advanced that there has not been "DIKAIOS ness" in his or her case.

**Thinking From God's Point Of View**

As we seek to relate this to thinking, two strains of meaning predominate. First, we see in this word thinking that comes from a completely just or fair base. The child that screams, "Not fair" is frequently doing it from a selfish position. John expresses it with a slightly different slant,

"You, dear children, are from God and have overcome them, because the one who is in you is greater than the one who is in the world. They are from the world and therefore speak from the viewpoint of the world, and the world listens to them. We are from God, and whoever knows God listens to us; but whoever is not from God does not listen to us. This is how we recognize the Spirit of truth and the spirit of falsehood." (I John 4:4-6)

The world speaks from the world's point of view. God's people should be thinking and speaking from God's point of view. By definition that will be fair and just.

It is at this point that I derive tremendous comfort from verses like Ephesians 1:11-12:

> "In Him we were also chosen, having been predestined according to the plan of Him who works out everything in conformity with the purpose of His Will, in order that we, who were the first to hope in Christ, might be for the praise of His glory."

Here I see that God has worked out everything in conformity with the purpose of His Will. He's in control! He's never caught by surprise by what we do. He doesn't wring His Hands in despair over things gone awry. He's worked out not *some* things, or even *most* things, but *all* things in conformity with the purpose of His Will.

And the purpose is that we might be the praise of His glory. He controls everything so that I might bring praise to Him. So then the song is true. He does have not only the whole world in His Hands - He has me in His hands. Things don't happen willy-nilly. I don't have to have a "Que sera sera" approach to life. No, my life is in the hands of a loving and just God who is in control of every event.

### God's Way - The Right Way

A second strain of meaning of the word DIKAIOS is seen in a recent commercial for a cereal. In the commercial, grandfatherly Will Brimley concludes that eating this oat cereal is "the right thing to do." The second meaning that emerges from a study of this word "right" is that of doing the right thing, the God-approved thing.

A major theme picked up in Scripture frequently is the matter of choosing the right way. Proverbs 14:12 points out, "There is a way that seems right to a man, but in the end it leads to death." and Jesus makes this additional statement in His Sermon on the Mount:

"Enter through the narrow gate for wide is the gate and broad is the road that leads to destruction, and many enter through it. But small is the gate and narrow the road that leads to life, and only a few find it (Matthew 7:13-14)."

A concluding thought is given us in I John 3:7-8,

"Dear children, do not let anyone lead you astray. He who does what is right is righteous. He who does what is sinful is of the devil, because the devil has been sinning from the beginning."

The message of Scripture is clear. There is a right way - God's way. There is a wrong way. That way is variously called 'man's way, 'our' way, the 'world's' way, even 'Satan's' way." All these ways may seem right, but they are sinful and lead to destruction and spiritual death. So then, occupying our minds, by planning and deciding the proper way to go, is certainly a godly thinking pattern.

Gary Friesen has shown how we can use wisdom in finding God's will for us in his book Decision Making And The Will Of God. He shows that frequently signs and circumstances and other determinations of God's will are really not valid, whereas Scripturally-based thinking patterns can validly be used. So then if I train my mind to think in Biblically-based ways, I can use it to help me know right ways when God's Word is not definite. I can exercise my mind in determining what is the right way to go. Well, this is right thinking.

Now let's see how to replace evil thinking with right thinking.

### Right Thoughts As a Replacement For Hurtful Thoughts

Imagine yourself in the middle of a protracted conflict. There have been heated exchanges, but now there is a lull in the battle. What is going on in your mind? Often you rehearse the arguments. Sometimes darker thoughts of belittlement, even hatred, add their evil presence. At these times, your mind whirls with evil activity.

How can this tide be reversed? I think Carole Mayhall in Words That Hurt, Words That Heal, points us in the right direction,

> "When we are hurt deeply, it is time to stop and examine both the reason for the pain and the purpose of God in that pain. If it's meant for good; if the bottom line is that God has allowed it in His kindness (ugly and hurtful as the process may have been) to perfect and hone us to be more like Jesus and to prepare us for a more fruitful life and for eternity; if we believe that, then we will accept it with a pure heart and clear conscience and without quarrel."

What I must do is to reverse my mental course by seeing that my current conflict is part of God's loving plan for me. I need to plan the right way for me to handle this situation. What would Jesus do if He were in my place? What can I do that will most honor Jesus? These thoughts could totally turn my thinking from sinful to right.

It takes the right viewpoint, and Charles Swindoll in Season of Life, sums it up,

"Pearls are the product of pain. For some unknown reason, the shell of the oyster gets pierced and an alien substance - a grain of sand slips inside. On the entry of that foreign irritant, all the resources within the tiny, sensitive oyster rush to the spot and begin to release healing fluids that otherwise would have remained dormant. By and by the irritant is covered and the wound is healed - by a pearl. No other gem has so fascinating a history. It is the symbol of stress - a healed wound...a precious, tiny jewel conceived through irritation, born of adversity, nursed by adjustments. Had there been no wounding, no irritating interruption, there could have been no pearl. Some oysters are never wounded... and those who seek for gems toss them aside, fit only for stew.

No wonder our heavenly home has as its entrance pearly gates! Those who go through them need no explanation. They are the ones who have been wounded, bruised, and have responded to the sting of irrationality with the pearl of adjustment."

### Right Thinking Replaces Pride

We have seen that the foundation for all evil thinking is pride, so if we assault that fortress, we can make real progress in the arena of the mind. Sunshine Magazine has printed these anonymous remarks:

"The desire to be well thought of makes people reluctant to say no to anyone regarding anything. We should cultivate an ability to say no to activities for which we have no time, no talent, and in which we have no interest or real concern. If we learn to say no to many things, then we will be able to say yes to things that matter most."

The need is to see plainly what God has called me to do.
There are profitable thoughts. When I see this clearly, I
can then choose the things to do that will help me achieve
the goals that God has called me to reach. I can set my
mind to this sort of planning. As I do this, the proud
thoughts that arise when I don't "say no to anyone
regarding anything" will be replaced by being "able to say
yes to things that matter most."

## Right Thinking Replaces Worry

Finally, right thinking can displace worry. This is quite
obvious. One feature of worry is that it divides the mind.
James 1:5-8 makes this clear,

> "If any of you lacks wisdom, he should ask God, who
> gives generously to all without finding fault, and it will
> be given to him. But when he asks, he must believe
> and not doubt, because he who doubts is like a wave
> of the sea, blown and tossed by the wind. That man
> should not think he will receive anything from the
> Lord: he is a double-minded man unstable in all he
> does."

Worry is a lack of trust, a doubting. One moment the
worrier thinks this, the next moment, that. He vacillates
from one viewpoint to the next. This can be corrected only
if the worrier will determine what is right, commit himself
to that course, and go for it with his whole heart. This is
what Paul meant when he makes this exhortation:

> "And whatever you do, whether in word or deed, do it
> all in the name of the Lord Jesus, giving thanks to God
> the Father through him." (Colossians 3:17).

He concludes:

"Whatever you do, work at it with all your heart, as working for the Lord, not for men, since you know that you will receive an inheritance from the Lord as a reward.    It is the Lord Christ you are serving." (Colossians 3:23-24).

So then, right thinking focuses on God's uprightness and fairness and doing the right thing to please Him.   It is a significant deterrent to evil thinking.   Our next target is the fourth word in the Philippians 4:8 text - pure.

# CHAPTER 12

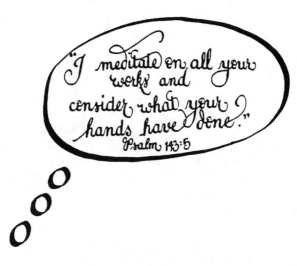

99 and 44/100 per cent pure

David was a man after God's own heart, but was severely handicapped after he allowed impure thoughts to captivate him. His palace was set on the top of a ridge. The ground fell away steeply to a gully and then rose more gradually where hundreds of homes were built. As David walked on the roof of his palace, he could see the roofs of many homes. One day his gaze fell upon a woman bathing out in the open. He could have spun on his heels and gotten away, but he stayed, and looked. As his stare continued, his pure thoughts changed over to thoughts of desire. The story is told in 2 Samuel 11. We learn from verse 2 that Bathsheba was very beautiful. David's impure thinking led him first to adultery, then to covering up and murder, and finally to sad consequences; the sword would never depart from his house (2 Samuel 12:10).

Kent and Barbara Hughes describe it this way in their book, Liberating Ministry From The Success Syndrome:

"From here on David's reign went downhill, despite his laudable repentance. Here are the terrible facts. His baby died. Then his beautiful daughter, Tamar, was raped by her half-brother Amnon. In turn, Amnon was murdered by Tamar's full-brother Absalom. Absalom so came to hate his father David for his moral turpitude that he led a rebellion under the tutelage of Bathsheba's resentful grandfather, Ahithophel."

David reversed the proper process with disastrous results. He replaced pure thinking (a man after God's own heart) with impure thinking (coveting Uriah's wife - Bathsheba). The proper process is to replace evil thinking with the kinds of thinking listed in Philippians 4:8. The word we come to now is pure thinking.

## Pure Thinking - What It Is

There is a very real sense in which it is easier to identify impure thinking than pure thinking. The Greek word is HAGNOS. It is defined as pure in the sense of undefiled, stained or mixed with sin. It is difficult to picture it. When you remove the sin, what's left? What's left is pure, unadulterated holiness. HAGIOS is the Greek word for holiness, and it is closely related to HAGNOS.

Genesis 39:6-12 helps us to see the similarities and differences of these two words. The narrative reads,

> "So he left in Joseph's care everything he had; with Joseph in charge, he did not concern himself with anything except the food he ate.
>
> Now Joseph was well-built and handsome, and after a while his master's wife took notice of Joseph and said, 'Come to bed with me!'
>
> But he refused. 'With me in charge,' he told her, 'my master does not concern himself with anything in the house; everything he owns he has entrusted to my care. No one is greater in this house than I am. My master has withheld nothing from me except you, because you are his wife. How then could I do such a wicked thing and sin against God?' And though she spoke to Joseph day after day, he refused to go to bed with her or even be with her.
>
> One day he went into the house to attend to his duties, and none of the household servants was inside. She caught him by his cloak and said, 'Come to bed with me!' But he left his cloak in her hand and ran out of the house."

Joseph was concerned about God's holiness. When he was presented with this temptation, he fled. HAGIOS (holiness) meant separating himself from the unholy fellowship with Potiphar's wife. HAGNOS meant keeping his own body pure and sinless.

In Titus 1:15 Paul makes a statement on purity that helps us to see what it does for our thinking,

> "To the pure, all things are pure, but to those who are corrupted and do not believe, nothing is pure. In fact, both their minds and consciences are corrupted."

This is real liberation! Think of it! All things are pure to those who are pure, but corrupt consciences and minds come as the automatic results of impure thinking. That's bondage! As long as David's thinking was marked by purity, he was free to live to God's glory; but after his affair with Bathsheba he was hampered as much as a hamstrung horse is unable to move about freely. However, when our mindset and motives are pure, we are free. We are far less apt to fall into temptations that trigger evil thinking. We can think about almost anything in a way that pleases God. Now let's identify some pure thinking patterns.

### Filling Your Mind With Thoughts of God

This really sounds great, doesn't it? But filling your mind with thoughts of God is not easy. I have to train my mind to do this. Maybe before the fall, Adam could just naturally conjure up thoughts of God, but since the fall, it isn't natural for many, if not all of us. I have needed a structure with some categories to help me to think about God in a profitable way.

Not too long ago, recognizing the necessity to think about God, I would say to myself, "You need to think

about God." When I tried, a few concepts floated in; such
as, God's holiness or sovereignty or goodness and love,
but then, all too soon, my mind would go blank, and I'd be
thinking about something else.

Eventually I settled on a pattern that has helped me
stay on track. Here it is:

*Monday:* Think about how you know that God is.
What has happened during your week where God has
been personally involved in your life? What Scripture
has spoken of Him meaningfully?

*Tuesday:* Think about what God is like. There are
attributes of God that we can't understand fully. These
attributes I like to think about and praise Him for.
These are qualities like His eternality (God has always
been and always will be), His omnipotence (He can do
anything He wills), His omnipresence(He can be
anywhere He wills), and His omniscience (He knows
everything).

*Wednesday:* Think about what God is like again.
Some attributes of God we understand a little better:
His holiness, His goodness, His love, His mercy, His
justice, His wrath, His jealousy. My goal is to bring
these to mind and consider them in the light of
Scripture   and then praise Him for them.

*Thursday:* Think about what God has made. His
creative acts bring many things to my mind. Not only
are there natural things like trees and scenic wonders
and animals, but also the mind of man. Just today, as
I write this, I thank God for wood that can be used for
so many things.

*Friday:* Think about what God has promised. As
you read Scripture take note of promises. Friday could

be a time to thank Him for several promises after you let your mind run on their meaning.

*Saturday:* Think about what God has done for you. What has He done for you personally this week? What has He done for you that the Bible has revealed? What has He given you? What are your gifts and talents? Thank Him for all this.

*Sunday:* Think about what He has done for your church. What is special about it? Who are some of the gifted people? What special things has He done for your church? Thank Him.

David's words in Psalm 143:5b give us his example: "I meditate on all your works and consider what your hands have done."

In I Samuel 12:24 we have part of what Samuel said in his farewell to the people he served so faithfully, "But be sure to fear the Lord and serve Him faithfully with all your heart; consider what great things He has done for you."

Finally, God Himself told Job, "Listen to this, Job; stop and consider God's wonders." (Job 37:14).

All these combine to encourage us to spend very profitable time in thinking the most pure thoughts one could think - thoughts of God. Now let's consider two examples of how pure thinking can replace evil thinking.

**Pure Thinking Melts Away Worry**

If worry were to be a sickness, the perfect medicine would be a healthy dose of God's promises. In those times when worry attacks, keep your mind pure by concentrating on what God has promised.

Kent Hughes relates this experience in Liberating Ministry From The Success Syndrome:

"New beginnings in the pastorate are traumatic for
any pastor and family. Suddenly he has a whole new
sea of faces and names to learn - and to love. He
wonders if his children are going to be accepted by
those in the youth group. If not, there is nowhere else
for them to go. He does not know whether the people
will like his preaching, or how his leadership style will
be accepted. Quite simply, he wonders if he and the
congregation will 'click'.

I felt all these pressures and concerns in the
beginning, and only my wife knew what I was dealing
with. At least I thought she was the only one. There
was someone else, however - Bob Noles, the West
Coast Representative for Wheaton College - who had
recommended me for the job, a man with pastoral
experience himself.

Bob invited me to lunch at a local restaurant, and
there, after some gentle probing, he said in his warm
pastoral way, 'Kent I want to share a verse with you
that has meant so much to Renee and me', and he
opened his Bible to Jeremiah 29:11 and read these
words: 'For I know the plans I have for you,' declares
the Lord, 'plans for welfare and not for calamity, to give
you a future and a hope.' " (NASB)

From these words, Bob Noles assured me that
whatever came, whether severity or goodness God had
plans for my welfare. I took this verse to my heart in
those early months. It has become dear to all my
thinking and my outlook on life."

Professional, semi-pro and even amateur worriers would
do well to copy down promises of God as they read their
Bibles. These could be kept in a handy place and be
committed to memory for instant use. Then when anxiety
attacks, the biblical repair and replacement kit will be
available.

## Pure Thinking Chases Away Lust

One of the first passages of the Bible I ever memorized was Psalm 119:9-11, but at first I didn't see something that is very helpful in countering lust.   Here is the passage:

"How can a young man keep his way pure? By living according to your word. I seek you with all my heart; do not let me stray from your commands.  I have hidden your word in my heart that I might not sin against you."

Verse 9 asks, "How can a young man keep his way pure?" Part of the answer is found in verse 11 when he states, "I have hidden your word in my heart that I might not sin against you." The purpose of hiding the word (memorizing) is that I won't sin, and verse 9, seems to indicate the sin would often be impurity.   So then scripture memorization is a way of warding off impure thoughts and replacing them with pure, scriptural thoughts.

Several times, I have taken on Scripture memorization projects, but recently, I have been working on the small book of I John. As soon as I had memorized the ten verses of the first chapter, I found that I could ward off lustful thinking by immediately reviewing that chapter again and again.  By the time I've struggled through it, the other thoughts are gone. This takes some preparation, but it is very effective.

# CHAPTER 13

## "Wouldn't It Be Loverly"

"And let us consider
how we may spur one another on
toward love and good deeds."

Hebrews 10:24

The fifth word which describes the godly-thinking package is lovely. My dictionary defines lovely as,

"having those qualities that inspire love, affection, or admiration; specifically, (a) beautiful; exquisite; (b) morally or spiritually attractive; gracious; (c) [Colloquially] highly enjoyable; as, a lovely party."

Yet when most people use this word, they think of beauty.

Eliza Doolittle, that delightful character from My Fair Lady, coined a word in a song that if taken in a literal way might capture the sense of this word for us. When dreaming of how life could be, she sang, "Wouldn't it be loverly." If this nice thing and that wonderful thing happened, it would be loverly. But the Greek word points us toward what relates to love and affection (loverly) more than what relates to beauty and happiness (lovely).

The Greek word is PROSPHILE. It is made up of a word PROS which means "toward" or "in the direction of" and PHILE, a word which describes a mutual love. The result of the composite word is "toward love." The basic idea when applied to thinking is a thought which is toward love - planning or concentration which will bring about a loving act.

**Roadblocks to Lovely Thinking**

Among the many roadblocks to this very spiritually healthy kind of thinking are two that I want to examine.

The first is modern American culture. Our typical concept
of love is far different from the biblical view.

An exchange from West Side Story illustrates the
modern American view. This musical is in an ethnic gang
war setting. Anita is pleading with Maria in song to give
up Tony because she wants Maria to "stick to your own
kind," and because Tony murdered Maria's brother.
Maria sings, "I hear your words and in my head I know
they're smart. But my heart, Anita, knows they're wrong."
She goes on, "I have a love and its all that I have. Right or
wrong - what else can I do." This song eloquently states
the case that one "falls in love." One can't help it. It is a
matter of the heart and one's feelings, and that's it. It
most certainly isn't a matter of the will. By the end of the
song Anita is convinced, and even though it was her lover
that was murdered by Tony, they sing together, "When
love comes so strong, there is no right or wrong. your love
is - your love."

Anthony Campolo makes the point well in Who Switched
The Price Tags:

> "In our romantically oriented culture, we are
> socialized to believe that love is an irrational emotion
> over which we have no control. Love, we are told, is
> something into which we 'fall'. And everyone is led to
> believe that when a person 'falls in love', he or she can
> expect to live happily ever after.
>
> It is no wonder that so many marriages fail. People
> don't understand that it entails hard work to maintain
> love, and that love is not a natural happening. They
> do not take hold of the fact that love is something we
> are called to do, and that love requires commitment,
> concern and concentration."

Since we believe that love comes naturally, we don't
work at it, or plan, or concentrate on it. After all, that's not
doing what comes naturally. Philippians 4:8 tells us,

however, to occupy our minds with thinking that is towards love.

The second roadblock to lovely thinking is laziness. I have found that loving involves hard work. Loving a wife means, among other things, meeting her needs, and many husbands haven't even taken the time to find out what their wives' needs are. More than a few think that because they have provided a large house, her own car, an insurance policy and enough labor saving devices that she requires a B.S. in Mechanical Engineering to operate her household, they have covered all the bases, and/or should be satisfied. They are blissfully ignorant that she is probably crying out, that he hasn't even scratched the surface.

Most women have a deep desire for intimate conversation, and meeting this need requires that the husband ask her intelligent questions and answer her when she probes him. But this involves work, and many men opt for the blank-eyed stare of the couch potato, and consequently their wives are unfulfilled.

**Lovely Thinking Fleshed Out**

Hebrews 10:24 points the way to lovely thinking, "And let us consider how we may spur one another toward love and good deeds." Notice, we are to consider how to spur others to love and good deeds. The word for consider means an intensified, hard thinking. The gears of our minds should be whirring as we seek to come up with plans for our own loving acts and how we might even help others to use their gifts and abilities in loving acts.

Jack Mayhall relates this story,

"I couldn't believe what I'd just heard. The group of young adults in our car had been laughing uproariously over some story that had been told when one of the women said wistfully, 'I can never remember a time in my growing up years when as a family, we ever laughed together'."

Loving thoughts for a parent can mean planning a family night. As our children were growing up, we set aside one night a week as a family night. One scenario that could have happened is this:

Kids:       "What're we gonna do?"
Father:     "I dunno. Whaddya wanna do?"  Then follows the endless, often fruitless, whaddya debate. The night can be ruined by argument and indecision.

On the other hand, loving thinking plans whiffleball on the beach, bike rides, miniature golf, special shows on TV with discussions afterwards on the good and bad things we saw, sailboating, and virtually anything else that we could figure out. It takes planning, prior arranging, and working things out in advance. It means taking the suggestions of the kids and figuring out ways to make them work. These are loving thoughts!

John Edmund Haggai has some other suggestions:

"Perhaps the Lord will lead you to do the washing for the lady next door who has been hampered by her day-and-night care of sick children. Perhaps you will contact the head of some fine Christian college or one of our seminaries to secure the name of a student who is in great need. You will help him. You may be led to invite a serviceman to have dinner with you on Sunday (we are not as thoughtful along that line as we were during the war years). There is no point in my going on, you take it from here."

Now I'd like to offer some ideas about how lovely thinking can replace some sinful thoughts.

## Perfect Love Drives Out Fear

First John 4:18 is part of one of the Scripture's fullest statements on love. It affirms,

> "There is no fear in love. But perfect love drives out fear, because fear has to do with punishment. The one who fears is not made perfect in love."

This is very significant! I fear because I think I'll get hurt through some punishment. So if I am afraid to speak to someone, it is often because I am focusing on his possible responses to me, rather than focusing on his needs. If I can zero in on his needs rather than worrying about rejection or other bad responses, these loving thoughts will drive out fear.

This is a big source of fearful thoughts. Often worriers will mull over all sorts of ways people could respond to them. Instead, we need to plan approaches to people. I like Bob Larsen's illustration. He compares people to Pacific Islands with coral reefs around them. We need to row around these islands until we find a way through the reefs. Most times we'll find a break in the guards people put up.

## Perfect Love Drives Out Self-pity

Several things had gone against a leader in a small church. Then he decided to step into a real den of wolves - the Youth Sunday School class. They chewed him up, and he quit everything. He told his pastor, "I'm just going to lay low for a while and lick my wounds." What was

going through his mind? The symptoms add up to a major
case of debilitating self-pititus.

Now can self-pity be replaced by lovely thoughts?
Anthony Campolo describes how it happened in the life of
one young woman:

> "I know of a young woman who lacked any
> semblance of joy in her life, even though she had
> accepted Christ as her Saviour. She lived a life of
> relative piety and went to church on Sundays with fair
> regularity. Nevertheless, life was depressing for her
> and she seemed bored with it. She went to a Christian
> psychotherapist for help, but after several sessions
> with him, felt that the effort was futile. Then one day
> she came into her therapist's office with her face
> radiant with excitement. 'I've had the most wonderful
> day,' she said. 'This morning I could not get my car
> started, so I called the pastor and asked him if he
> could drive me to my appointment with you. He said
> he would, but on the way he had to stop by the
> hospital and make a few calls. I went with him and
> while I was in the hospital, I visited some elderly
> people in one of the wards. I read from the Bible and
> prayed with them. By the time the morning was over, I
> was higher than a kite. I haven't felt this good in
> years.'
>
> The psychotherapist quickly responded, 'Now we
> know how to make you happy! Our problem is solved!
> Now we know how to keep you out of the doldrums!'
>
> Much to his surprise, the young woman answered,
> 'You don't expect me to do this sort of thing every day,
> do you?' "

The psychotherapist saw that the way out of her
depression was the doing of loving acts. As depression
which often holds hands with self-pity can be replaced by

love, so planning out the loving act can replace the thought of self-pity. Unfortunately this young woman refused to take the key to unlock her depression.


**Perfect Love Drives Out Hurtful Thoughts**

John's first epistle reminds me of the short staccato burst of automatic weapons fire, and his bullets go right to the heart of the matter. First John 2:9-11 is an example:

"Anyone who claims to be in the light but hates his brother is still in the darkness. Whoever loves his brother lives in the light, and there is nothing in him to make him stumble. But whoever hates his brother is in the darkness and walks around in the darkness; he does not know where he is going, because the darkness has blinded him."

Verse 10 is of real interest. The one who loves his brother has nothing in him to make him stumble. How can loving my brother prevent me from stumbling?

I once worked with a sizable group of single young adults who were also very young Christians. The whole question of stumbling was always good for lively discussion. The word gives us the picture of being tripped much as one person will stick his foot out to trip up another person. Well, these folks were always accusing one another of causing them to stumble. I even heard one say with somewhat less than perfect use of the English language, "You stumbled me." Translation: "You did something that made me sin." There was certainly a lack of facing up to his own bad choices. After all, no one made him sin. Furthermore, he was trying to shift the blame to the one he claims made him stumble.

This kind of thing can also lead to going over all the bad things others have done - hurtful thoughts again. When we catch ourselves, we can let lovely thoughts reverse our mental engines. If my mind is deeply involved in how I can minister to someone, I am not going to be personally affected by his shortcomings, mistakes and sins. If I love him, I won't stumble over what he does. This is one thing the Bible means when it says, "Love covers a multitude of sins."

We now progress on to the sixth word - admirable.

# CHAPTER 14

## THE DESIGN AND MANUFACTURE OF A WARM FUZZY

"Far too noisy, my dear Mozart.

Far too many notes."

Two prisoners shared a small cell with a window three feet over their heads. They spoke eloquently of the stark reality of their present life. As they looked at that window, one man focused on the iron bars. He was confined, and his life was bleak and hopeless. His cellmate looked through the bars and concentrated on the stars. They told him of a future of freedom and hope. One's life was painted in the various hues of the gray bars; the other, in the fire of the stars. So much depends upon our focus.

The sixth word in Philippians 4:8 is admirable. It is EUPHEMA in the original. EU is a word that means good, and PHEMA means report or news, hence good report or good news. The kind of thinking referred to is thinking that searches for the good rather than the bad in another. This kind of thinking is rare indeed and possibly merits being put on an "endangered species" list.

### The Opposite of Fault-Finding

A Munich schoolmaster reportedly dismissed his ten-year-old student with the words, "You will never amount to very much." Such put-downs are common; sometimes the prophet is correct, but in this case, the student was Albert Einstein.

One magazine sought to ironically forestall fault-finding this way:

"Just in case you find any mistakes in this magazine, please remember they were put there for a purpose. We try to offer something for everyone. Some people are always looking for mistakes and we didn't want to disappoint you!"

Faultfinding has been going on for a long time as Daniel can bear witness:

"It pleased Darius to appoint 120 satraps to rule throughout the kingdom, with three administrators over them, one of whom was Daniel. The satraps were made accountable to them so that the king might not suffer loss.   Now Daniel so distinguished himself among the administrators and the satraps by his exceptional qualities that the king planned to set him over the whole kingdom.   At this, the administrators and the satraps tried to find grounds for charges against Daniel in his conduct of government affairs, but they were unable to do so. They could find no corruption in him, because he was trustworthy and neither corrupt nor negligent. Finally these men said 'We will never find any basis for charges against this man Daniel unless it has something to do with the law of his God.' " (Daniel 6:1-5).

Although these men turned over every rock in Daniel's life, they couldn't find any corruption, but they knew they had struck pay dirt when they considered Daniel's obedience to the law of his God.   It reminds me of the modern fault-finders who checked into Supreme Court nominee Robert Bork's video rentals.   They were, no doubt, deeply disappointed when they found only PG's and G's rather than the X's and R's they so eagerly sought. These were all skilled practitioners in the art of faultfinding.

And yet, most of us aren't far behind them.  Once when I was working with a couple trying to ward off an almost inevitable divorce, I asked the husband to try to find twenty things about his wife that were good.   As I explained that I meant any quality, trait, characteristic or act of hers that he thought was good, I could easily observe her good characteristics myself. I could see that the house was kept immaculately, that the meals she cooked were very good, (his expanding belly was ample evidence of that), that she was a fine mother, and that she dressed herself in an attractive manner. I thought that the assignment was going to be a "piece of cake." A week later, he had only seen three good things, and he claimed to have tried hard! This same man, however, had presented me with a seemingly endless list of her faults not long before. Although he may be an extreme case, I have found many following his example.

**Why Do We Do It?**

The perversity of pride that lurks in all of us does not want to see other people get ahead of us. If we perceive that someone else has by his character or acts risen above us in the eyes of others (Figure 1a), then we will often find fault with him so that we can bring him down to our level (Figure 1b).

A truly aggressive campaign of fault-finding may actually get me to appear better than him (Figure 1c).

Figure 1

| Figure 1a | Figure 1b | Figure 1c |
|---|---|---|
| Him | | |
| | ↓ | ↓ |
| Me | Him  Me | Me |
| | | ↓ |
| | | Him |

This perverseness is also seen in the fact that we often find fault at the very point of our own weakness. Because we see the fault so clearly in ourselves, it jumps out at us when we see it in others. This little couplet sums it up:

> "Things that thou dost in others see, are the most prevalent in thee."

## The Need For "Warm Fuzzies"

Shad Helmstetter has calculated that over the period of time from birth until he leaves home, a child hears things like "It can't be done," or "It is impossible," or "You shouldn't do it" 148,200 times. What a legacy to start life in the big wide world!

William James of Harvard believed, "The deepest principle in human nature is the craving to be appreciated." I think he is on to something because we are commanded by Philippians 4:8 to think admirable thoughts. "Warm fuzzies" is a wonderful description of a compliment, and our minds should be a breeding ground for warm fuzzies. This is the kind of fuzzy thinking which should be done by all.

Charles Sheed makes it his goal to pay his wife one sincere compliment each day. What would it be like to be on the receiving end of one sincere compliment a day? It would take all the droop out of a droopy face. This is a big part of what Proverbs 3:27 means: "Do not withhold good from those who deserve it, when it is in your power to act."

I had been a Christian a couple of years and was the youth leader of our church. Our pastor, Ron Mahurin, usually spoke when our youth group went to a nursing home. On one occasion, he was unable to be there on the day we were scheduled. I was going over with him about who could speak at that service when he said, "You do it. You've got something to say." Possibly Proverbs 20:5 was in his mind, which states: "The purposes of a man's heart are deep waters, but a man of understanding draws them out. In any case, he was thinking about things that I could do that I was not so sure I could do. It was one of the things that God used to point me into the ministry.

## Developing Admirable Mental Snapshots

The first thing we must do in the development of admirable thoughts is to ask, "What is my focus?" Am I focusing in on faults or am I searching for good points?

**Figure 2**

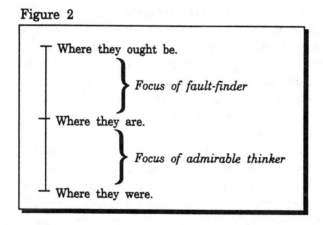

This diagram may help in finding your focus. In Figure 2, I have diagramed the fact that although everyone's goal is to be like Christ (Where they ought to be), the reality is that everyone falls short of that goal (Where they are). Someone is improving in a given area, but there is still a long way to go. If you focus on all the things that still must be done, you have a fault-finder focus. If you focus on the ground that has been gained, that is admirable thinking.

When healthy criticism is balanced by admirable thinking, faults can be corrected and progress can be noted, but otherwise there is much less motivation to change. Frustration is inevitably produced by an unbalanced and constant criticism.

What is your focus? Do you usually see faults? Do you, while noting the faults, also give credit and praise for improvements?


**Replacing Hurtful Thoughts**

Once the focus of your thinking has been determined, you can begin to make the necessary changes. Recently a friend of mine did something that gave me reason to question a choice that he had made. It started a cycle of negative thinking within me, and soon I was mentally rehearsing all the faults that came to my mind about that person. Suddenly, I recognized I was in the middle of a growing hurtful thought pattern, and I had to make a decision. Was I going to go on, or was I going to stop? I decided to stop, but I had to replace those hurtful thoughts. I deliberately started to mentally list that friend's many good points. After a while, I found that I was completely out of the hurtful thought cycle. I was thinking admirable thoughts in the place of the hurtful ones. How much better the day went after that!

If replacing hurtful thoughts is necessary for you, then I can recommend this approach. First, recognize your hurtful thought pattern. Then determine to stop. Finally, either in your mind (good) or on paper (better), list the admirable qualities of the person you've been mentally assaulting.

## Replacing Self-Pity

Sometimes specialists in self-pity believe others cause their problems. On one occasion, I worked with a woman whose husband was not coming close to being the kind of husband God called him to be. This woman was discouraged and chock full of self-pity. When asked her to spend a bit of time in the next week considering all her husband's good points, she really went to work. She came back with a list of great characteristics and talents. It was the turning point in their relationship. She changed her focus, and her whole attitude toward him changed. Self-pity evaporated!

Sometimes people take a hard look at themselves and say, "Phooey, I don't like what I see." In this case, self-pity is directed inward. Several times I have asked people with this struggle to write down all the things they do well, all their good personality traits, all the good physical qualities, all the good things about their family situation and so on. When they have done this, they have had a completely different view of their Creator. The result of this realignment of thinking has been peace and joy.

# CHAPTER 15

## Putting Your Best Mind Forward

> Quality is remembered long after price is forgotten.
>
> — Stanley Marcus, merchandising expert

Someone asked the team of astronauts who were busily preparing for lift-off,

"Well, how does it feel?" One of them answered with a smile, "It really makes you think twice when you realize everything in this entire project was constructed according to the lowest bid."

This, I'm afraid, is a way of life to many people. Their way of thinking and way of living is "according to the lowest bid."

The seventh word in Philippians 4:8 is "excellent". Our minds are to dwell on excellent thoughts. Let's turn our attention to what this means.


## Giving It Our Best

A sportscaster by the name of Joe Zone ends his broadcast by exhorting, "Give tomorrow your best shot." For the Christian, this means what Paul urged in Colossians 3:17, "And whatever you do, whether in word or deed, do it all in the name of the Lord Jesus, giving thanks to God the Father through him." Paul concludes a few verses later in verse 23,"Whatever you do, work at it with all your heart, as working for the Lord, not for men."

Solomon concurs in Ecclesiastes 9:10: "Whatever your hand finds to do, do it with all your might, for in the grave, where you are going, there is neither working nor planning nor knowledge nor wisdom."

The Bible message is clear. Do your best. I was struck by this story that was related by Charles Swindoll:

"For many years Admiral Hyman Rickover was the head of the United States Nuclear Navy. His admirers and his critics held strongly opposing views about the stern and demanding admiral. For many years every officer aboard a nuclear submarine was personally interviewed and approved by Rickover. Those who went through those interviews usually came out shaking in fear, anger, or total intimidation. Among them was ex-President Jimmy Carter who, years ago, applied for service under Rickover. This is his account of a Rickover interview:

'I had applied for the nuclear submarine program, and Admiral Rickover was interviewing me for the job. It was the first time I met Admiral Rickover, and we sat in a large room by ourselves for more than two hours, and he let me choose any subjects I wished to discuss. Very carefully, I chose those about which I knew most at the time - current events, seamanship, music, literature, naval tactics, electronics, gunnery - and he began to ask me a series of questions of increasing difficulty. In each instance, he soon proved that I knew relatively little about the subject I had chosen.

He always looked right into my eyes, and he never smiled. I was saturated with cold sweat.

Finally, he asked a question and I thought I could redeem myself. He said, 'How did you stand in your class at the Naval Academy?' Since I had completed my sophomore year at Georgia Tech before entering Annapolis as a plebe, I had done very well, and I swelled my chest with pride and answered, 'Sir, I stood fifty-ninth in a class of 820!' I sat back to wait for the congratulations - which never came. Instead the question: 'Did you do your best?' I started to say, 'Yes, sir' but I remembered who this was and recalled several of the many times at the academy when I could have learned more about our allies, our enemies, weapons, strategy, and so forth. I was just human. I finally gulped and said, 'No, sir, I didn't always do my best.'

He looked at me for a long time, and then turned his chair around to end the interview. He asked one final question, which I have never been able to forget - or to answer. He said, 'Why not?' I sat there for a while, shaken, and then slowly left the room."

This really spoke to me. All through my days in elementary school it seems I got the same comments from my teachers in that little space in the report cards that was left for the teacher's remarks. Mine would frequently go something like this: "Johnny is doing fairly well, but he is not doing his best. He could do so much better." All the way through high school and on into college at the University of Tennessee, my motto must have been, "Just get by." At the end of my sophomore year, the powers that be at the University informed me my grades were too low. I had to spend two quarters at another school to get my grades up. This shocked me into doing better, but I still wasn't doing my best. A few years later when I became a Christian, I made a more Christ-like effort at studying when I went to Northeastern Bible College.

## Giving God the Best of our Best

Genesis 4:1-5 describes two brothers who chose to worship God in different ways. Cain brought "some of the fruits of the soil as an offering to the Lord:" In contrast Abel brought "fat portions from some of the firstborn of his flock." 'The Lord looked with favor on Abel and his offering, but on Cain and his offering he did not look with favor. " Why did God turn down Cain's offering? It seems likely that Cain had not given his best. He had possibly given bruised fruit, rotten fruit, or stunted fruit. Abel, however, had given his best.

I like the hymn that urges us, "Give of your best to the Master, give of the strength of your youth." Yet all too often God gets the dregs of our energy and effort. This is pointed out in Malachi 1:6-8,

> "A son honors his father, and a servant his master. If I am a father where is the honor due me? If I am a master, where is the respect due me?" says the Lord Almighty. 'It is you O priests, who show contempt for my name.'
> 'But you ask, How have we shown contempt for your name?'
> 'You place defiled food on my altar.' 'But you ask, 'How have we defiled you?'
> By saying that the Lord's table is contemptible. When you bring blind animals for sacrifice, is that not wrong? When you sacrifice crippled or diseased animals, is that not wrong? Try offering them to your governor! Would he be pleased with you? Would he accept you?", says the Lord Almighty."

In verse 7 God accuses His people of putting defiled food on His altar. How often the people of God give defiled food! I remember when I was a brand new Christian and a missionary had requested visual aid materials. Our church was rallying to the cry. Someone brought a large box of broken crayons. Most of the fragments were less than an inch long! It was defiled food.

Ronald Allen and Gordon Barrar in their book Worship, as they call for quality in worship, describe what happens too many times:

> "After a piano has seen better days, had a few keys broken, been left in the garage for a few years, been sideswiped by the car, sustained a cracked soundboard and several broken strings, it is given to

the church to be used in the service of the King of Kings!"

This is enacted multiplied times as people give God less than their best. In contrast to this, Exodus 23:19 cries out, "Bring the best of the firstfruits of your soil to the house of the Lord your God." No broken crayons or destroyed pianos are anywhere near good enough as acts of worship for the God of Heaven. Let's give it our best shot and of our best shots, let's give God our very best.

**Enemies of the Best**

Two very common things work against excellence. The first is lack of preparation. Malachi 1:8 challenges us to try our feeble offerings to God on our governor. "Would he be pleased with you? Would he accept you?" asks the Lord. Suppose President Bush announced that he was attending a certain church. Do you think the soloist might just work a little harder than usual? Do you think the pastor might really give it his best for that sermon?

This whole idea makes it clear that we often do not do our very best for the run-of-the-mill worship service. In fact, there should be no run-of-the-mill services. We are there to worship One who is higher than the President of the United States. We are there to worship the King of Kings! He merits our very best preparation!

A second enemy of excellence is dilutedness. Acts 6:1-4 narrates this event:

"In those days when the number of disciples was increasing, the Grecian Jews among them complained against those of the Aramaic-speaking community because their widows were being overlooked in the daily distribution of food. So the Twelve gathered all the disciples together and said, 'It would not be right for us to neglect the ministry of the Word of God in order to wait on tables. Brothers, choose seven men from among you who are known to be full of the Spirit and wisdom. We will turn this responsibility over to them and will give our attention to prayer and the ministry of the word.' "

The apostles did not claim, "Waiting on tables is beneath us." They were saying, "Our focus is to be on prayer and the ministry of the Word." They refused to dilute their ministry with so many worthwhile things and be "spread so thin" that they weren't doing anything really well.

The first real ministry Ruthie and I had after becoming Christians was overseeing the Youth Fellowship in our small church. It was our only ministry, and God was pleased to bless the work in many ways. As is often the case, we soon were doing several other jobs in the church. It was not long before we were not doing anything as well, because we didn't have the time to concentrate on the ministry God had given us. We weren't focused in on what we were doing. We were no longer doing our best because we were diluted and relatively ineffective.

How can I use excellent thinking to reverse evil thinking? Now that we understand to some extent what excellent thinking is, we can turn our attention to using it to replace certain kinds of sinful thinking.


## Excellent Thinking Replaces Self-Pity

Self-pitiers are also frequently afflicted with a less-than-wholesome pessimism. Sometimes they even make provision for failure by whining, "I'm too this or that," or "This has happened to me, so...," or "I have this problem, so...".

Dr. Stanton Samenow in Before It's Too Late hits a vein of truth,

"Yet, self-esteem is not raised by insight or talk alone, but by what a person does with his insights. It works the same way at school or on the job. A teacher can encourage or discourage a student but, in the final analysis, nothing boosts a student's self-image more than actually succeeding at something that has required hard work. For the most part, a person's view of his own worth depends not on his intentions, fantasies, or pretensions, but on what he actually accomplishes."

So confidence is gained more through performance than anything else. It sounds so incredibly simple. If I am pessimistic, then what I need to do is to start thinking about how I can do a better job at whatever I am doing. Then, I will be more confident because I am, in fact, doing better.

What areas of your life cause you to shudder when you stop for honest evaluation? Before you invite your friends to an old-fashioned pity party, spend some time meditating on how you can do it better, more creatively, or just differently. Innovation is usually very difficult because we have to think hard and overcome obstacles. It isn't easy but the rewards can be very fulfilling.

### Excellent Thinking Replaces Lust

I am not so sure how this works, but when my mind drifts into wanting something for myself, one of the most effective ways of turning it around is to force myself to think of areas of service for God. This procedure is seen in Psalm 1:1-2:

"Blessed is the man who does not walk in the counsel of the wicked or stand in the way of sinners or sit in the seat of mockers. But his delight is in the law of the Lord, and on his law he meditates day and night."

Consciously bringing my mind to consider what I soon will be doing for the Lord, whether it is a teaching time, message, counseling session, or program of any sort,is an effective antidote for poisonous lustful thinking.

Admiral Hyman Rickover asked the penetrating question, "Why not?" Jimmy Carter was left to wonder, "Indeed, why not?" As I understand the parable quoted below, God will ask the same question:

"Again, it will be like a man going on a journey, who called his servants and entrusted his property to them. To one he gave five talents of money, to another two talents, and to another one talent, each according to his ability. Then he went on his journey. The man who had received the five talents went at once and put his money to work and gained five more. So also, the one with the two talents gained two more. But the man who had received the one talent went off, dug a hole in the ground and hid his master's money.

After a long time the master of those servants returned and settled accounts with them. The man who had received the five talents brought the other five. 'Master,' he said, 'you entrusted me with five talents. See, I have gained five more.'

His master replied, 'Well done, good and faithful servant! You have been faithful with a few things; I will put you in charge of many things. Come and share your master's happiness!'

The man with the two talents also came. 'Master,' he said, 'you entrusted me with two talents; see, I have gained two more.'

His master replied, 'Well done, good and faithful servant! You have been faithful with a few things; I will put you in charge of many things.  Come and share your master's happiness!'

Then the man who had received the one talent came. 'Master,' he said, 'I knew that you are a hard man, harvesting where you have not sown and gathering where you have not scattered seed.  So I was afraid and went out and hid your talent in the ground.  See, here is what belongs to you.'

His master replied, 'You wicked lazy servant! So you knew that I harvest where I have not sown and gather where I have not scattered seed?  Well, then, you should have put my money on deposit with the bankers so that when I returned I would have received it back with interest.

Take the talent from him and give it to the one who has the ten talents.  For everyone who has will be given more, and he will have an abundance.  Whoever does not have, even what he has will be taken from him.  And throw that worthless servant outside, into the darkness, where there will be weeping and gnashing of teeth." (Matthew 25:14-30).

When God asks you, "What did you do with all I gave you?  Did you do your best?" What will you say?

# CHAPTER 16

# Last, but not Least

"For although they knew God, the neither glorified Him as God nor gave thanks to Him, but their thinking became futile and their foolish hearts were darkened."

ROMAN 1:21

We have been examining the eight words that describe what righteous thinking is to be like, and now we come to the last, but surely not the least. In fact, if any of these words could be a cure-all to evil thinking, this would be it! So this study before us is of great importance.

**Praiseworthy Thinking Delineated**

As I first looked at these words, a problem arose in my mind as to differentiating the sixth word, "admirable", and the eight word, "praiseworthy." Eventually it became clear to me that the difference must basically be found in the object of the thinking. Admirable thinking, as I see it, finds its object in other people, things, and events. It is the opposite of fault-finding. So it is thinking on the good of people, things and events around me. Praiseworthy thinking on the other hand, finds its object in God. It is thinking on the good qualities and actions of God.

As a kid the arrival of the Sears catalog was an eagerly-looked-for event. I would spend wide-eyed hours looking through the pictures of all the goods offered for sale. I remember the catalog often delineated the products by the descriptions:  good, better, best (I can't imagine: junk, cheap, adequate). Well, in the area of thinking, I have no doubt that praiseworthy thinking is best. It is a level higher than the rest.

**Praiseworthy Thinking Enjoined**

Scripture is full of commands and illustrations of praise. In the Psalms alone, the theme bursts forth so that even the most spiritually dull could hardly miss it. Just a few examples are:

*Psalm 33:1-3*
"Sing joyfully to the Lord, you righteous; it is fitting for the upright to praise Him. Praise the Lord with the harp; make music to Him on the ten-stringed lyre. Sing to Him a new song; play skillfully, and shout for joy."

*Psalm 34:1-3*
"I will extol the Lord at all times; His praise will always be on my lips. My soul will boast in the Lord; let the afflicted hear and rejoice. Glorify the Lord with me; let us exalt His name together."

*Psalm 150*
"Praise the Lord. Praise God in His sanctuary; praise Him in his mighty heavens. Praise Him for his acts of power; praise Him for his surpassing greatness. Praise Him with the sounding of the trumpet, praise Him with the harp and lyre, praise Him with tambourine and dancing, praise Him with the strings and flute, praise Him with the clash of cymbals, praise Him with resounding cymbals. Let everything that has breath praise the Lord. Praise the Lord."

I think, however, the most powerful statement in all of Scripture is found in Romans 1:21:

"For although they knew God, they neither glorified Him as God nor gave thanks to Him, but their thinking became futile and their foolish hearts were darkened."

Here we see the devastating results when we turn away from praise and thanksgiving. The heart that makes this choice is foolish. Thinking becomes futile, and ends in darkness. The light at the end of this tunnel really is an oncoming train. Foolishness, futility, and ultimate darkness - who would want it? Yet, so very many do. Praiseworthy thinking, on the other hand, carries us into the light of God.

## Praiseworthy Thinking Illustrated

The study of this word has caused me to seek to apply praiseworthy thinking in my own life. Since I was already keeping a journal of significant events and discussions of each day, it was not too difficult for me to begin to search for praiseworthy things seen every day. I would write "PTL" (Praise the Lord) after anything I considered praiseworthy. As I continued, I became more adept at seeing God's hand in my life, and even things I would have seen as bad before I would see as praiseworthy. Praising God begot more praising, because I saw more and more to praise.

There was a by-product. At the time I started this praise project, I also had some victories in my thought life battles. So then the PTL's were in themselves a PTL.

## Praiseworthy Thinking Replaces Lust

We are bombarded almost constantly with advertisements. They fly into our brains like automatic weapon bullets. Charles Swindoll has captured the idea:

"Shiny, slick, appealing print and pictures designed to hijack your concentration and kidnap your attention. Before you realize it, the Madison Avenue

Pied Piper has led you into a world of exaggerated make-believe, convincing you that you simply cannot live without...

- A new Polaroid camera stuffed with SX-70 film (that develops twice as fast!)
- An elegant diamond solitaire (a diamond is forever!)
- A Dodge Sportsman Wagon to pull your new outboard.
- A set of Firestone's finest.
- Carter's Little Pills 'specially coated to pass right through your stomach releasing their action only in your lower tract.'"

He goes on to point out that the aggregate result is to build up discontentment with our present state. The word for this is "lust". Lust flourishes in the soil of discontentment.

Paul crystallizes the opposite view in Philippians 4:11-13,

"I am not saying this because I am in need, for I have learned to be content whatever the circumstances. I know what it is to be in need, and I know what it is to have plenty. I have learned the secret of being content in any and every situation, whether well fed or hungry, whether living in plenty or in want. I can do everything through Him who gives me strength."

One of the best ways to develop this contentment is by praising God. It is an effective way to counteract the pangs of lust. When some desire for anything, whether a material or sexual object, begins, one successful reaction is to turn to a written or mental check list of praises. This should bring the contentment and peace that replaces lust.

## Praiseworthy Thinking Replaces Self-Pity

The focus of self-pity is how bad everything is for me.
The focus of praise is how good God is. These are obvious
mental opposites.

When you find yourself starting down the spiral
staircase of self-pity, follow Eddie Fisher's advice in he
song he made popular long ago, "When you're worried,
and you can't sleep, count your blessings instead of
sheep" There is the need for a conscious effort to stop,
turn around, and make a decision to start thinking
praiseworthy thoughts. Before long, you will find yourself
at the top of the stairs.

## Praiseworthy Thinking Replaces Pride

Now we take out our axe and take on the biggest, ugliest
tree in the forest of evil thinking - Pride. Again, our work
centers on Romans 1:18-23:

"The wrath of God is being revealed from heaven
against all the godlessness and wickedness of men
who suppress the truth by their wickedness, since
what may be known about God is plain to them,
because God has made it plain to them. For since the
creation of the world, God's invisible qualities - his
eternal power and divine nature - have been clearly
seen, being understood from what has been made, so
that men are without excuse.

For although they knew God, they neither glorified
Him as God nor gave thanks to Him, but their thinking
became futile and their foolish hearts were darkened.
Although they claimed to be wise, they became fools
and exchanged the glory of the immortal God for
images made to look like mortal man and birds and
animals and reptiles."

There is a sinful pattern here. There is a rejection of God. "Don't glorify Him. Don't give Him credit," they would cry out. In His place, they erect monuments to themselves. Self-worship replaces the proper worship of God. This is the way pride develops. Self-worship (pride) replaces the worship of God.

Here's how to turn this horrible pattern around: renounce yourself, recognize what God has done, and thank Him. Again, praise is the vehicle to put an end to the most vexing of the thought patterns.

Let me say just a few words about the mechanics of thinking praiseworthy thoughts. There must be preparation. Before the crunch of temptation comes, you must be ready. This can be done by your journal and the PTL's will help. But if you wait until the time when temptation is upon you, you may find yourself going to your bank of praise and finding nothing to withdraw. The bank of your mind might just be blank. So, be ready.

# CHAPTER 17

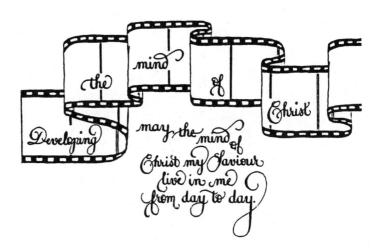

Developing the mind of Christ

may the mind of
Christ my Saviour
live in me
from day to day.

There is one concluding passage for us to consider and, in my opinion, it is the climax of our whole study. The passage is Philippians 2:3-11:

"Do nothing out of selfish ambition or vain conceit, but in humility consider others better than yourselves. Each of you should look not only to your own interests, but also to the interests of others.

Your attitude should be the same as that of Christ Jesus: Who being in very nature God, did not consider equality with God something to be grasped, but made Himself nothing, taking the very nature of a servant, being made in human likeness. And being found in appearance as a man, He humbled Himself and became obedient to death - even death on a cross!

Therefore God exalted Him to the highest place and gave Him the name that is above every name, that at the name of Jesus every knee should bow, in heaven and on earth and under the earth, and every tongue confess that Jesus Christ is Lord, to the glory of God the Father."

## The Foundation of Evil Thinking

First, note that selfish ambition is foundational to all sinful thinking (v.3). How often you hear people asserting, "I've got to do what's right for me." Pro athletes seem to specialize in this kind of remark. Selfish ambition is seen in lines: I wonder what percentage of customers stick with the "under ten items" for the express line in the super market. Selfish ambition is seen in the way people drive.

Living in the Northeast part of the United States, I get to
see many examples each day of people who risk their lives
(and the lives of others) to cut minutes off their daily
commute.

The amazing contrast to this is found in Jesus Christ as
Paul drives it home for us in verses 6-8,

> "Your attitude should be the same as that of Christ
> Jesus: Who, being in very nature God, did not consider
> equality with God something to be grasped, but made
> himself nothing, taking the very nature of a servant,
> being made in human likeness.
>
> And being found in appearance as a man, He
> humbled Himself and became obedient to death - even
> death on a cross!"

Unlike us, He was not grasping for His rights, but gave
them up. He voluntarily went from "out of the ivory
palaces into a world of woe." He voluntarily came to be
born in a smelly stable. We romanticize the manger to
make it seem nice, but in reality it was a place filled with
animal feces, rats, and mice. His death was anything but
romantic, but He voluntarily chose that death, not for His
benefit, but for ours.

### Jesus and Fearful Thinking

Fearful thinking is selfish in nature. When thinking
fearfully, we are whining, "What is going to happen to
me?" Our focus is on terrible possibilities that could
happen to us in the future. We lose sight of God and His
promises.

Compare that attitude with Jesus's attitude on the cross
as recorded in Luke 23:46, "Jesus called out with a loud
voice, 'Father, into your hands I commit my spirit.' " Here

in the greatest of crises', He completely trusted God. He put His whole spirit into God's hands.

Let's try to make this practical. How can we actually develop the mind of Christ and trust God, rather than crumbling in a heap of worry? This chart may be helpful.

*(See chart on next page)*

# Applying Philippians 4:8 to Fearful Thinking

*Fearful Thinking - Dwelling on What Might Happen*

| Replace With . . . | True Thinking | Right Thinking | Pure Thinking | Lovely Thinking |
|---|---|---|---|---|
| **What to Do:** | Thinking on things that are true as opposed to false and real as opposed to fake. | Thinking from God's point of view. | Filling your mind with thoughts of God. | Considering how you can give of yourself to someone. |
| **How This Helps:** | Worry often involves a kind of reverse fantasy focusing on all sorts of terrible consequences of the mind on reality and real solutions. | Vacillation is a typical feature of the fearful heart. Decisions are hard to make for fear of what might happen. When you determine this is the right way and this is how you will go, fear departs. | Since worry often imagines the worst of circumstances, filling your mind with the promises of God will crowd out that fear. | Since fear often concerns itself with the responses of others toward you, determination to love will overcome the fear of a bad response. |
| **Project:** | List in column 1 all the things you are currently worried about. In column 2 write down the real approach you should use to the problems presented. | List in Column 1 areas of indecisiveness. In Column 2 determine what God would have you to do about these things. | In daily devotions make a list of promises God makes. Begin to memorize those promises one by one. When worry comes, recite appropriate Bible passages and apply their meaning. | List in column 1 those people you are fearful of or uneasy with. In Column 2, design loving acts for each other. |

## Jesus and Hurtful Thinking

Selfish ambition rises to the surface when you think hurtfully. You think, "My rights have been violated," and you ask, "How can I get them back?" Or you may run others down in your mind. We must let the hurtful thoughts simmer on the back burner of our minds.

How different Jesus was! If there was ever anyone who could say, "My rights were violated," it was He. He was God, and puny men were taunting, mocking, hurting and spitting on Him. Who did these people think they were? How dare they? He had the power to strike back. As He had remarked,

"Do you think I cannot call on my Father, and He will at once put at my disposal more than twelve legions of angels?" (Matthew 26:53).

But when on the cross, His plea was very different, "Father forgive them, for they do not know what they are doing."

So, even then when it would almost be expected that He would strike back, He refused to act or think hurtfully. Instead, He cried out for forgiveness for them.

Here is a chart that can help us to transform our thinking from hurtful to Christlike:

*(See chart on next page)*

# Applying Philippians 4:8 to Hurtful Thinking

*Hurtful Thinking - Treasuring Negative Thoughts About Others or Plotting Revenge for Real or Imagined Hurts*

| Replace With . . . | Right Thinking | Lovely Thinking | Admirable Thinking |
|---|---|---|---|
| **What to Do:** | Thinking from God's point of view. | Considering how you can give of yourself to someone. | Reviewing the good characteristics and acts of others as opposed to fault-finding. |
| **How This Helps:** | Since hurtful thinking often involves going over the details of past arguments and rehearsing them for possible ways of improving our side, seeing God's point of view would replace these hurtful thoughts. | When mentally running someone down or plotting revenge, putting mental energy into loving acts will dissipate those hurtful thoughts. | Forcing yourself to make a list of someone's good qualities and actions will result in a deactivation of the hurtful thought process. |
| **Project:** | Set up (3) Columns. <br>1. Unresolved arguments which occupy your mind. <br>2. Your point of view in this dispute. <br>3. God's point of view in this dispute. | Set up (2) Columns. <br>1. All the people with whom you entertain hurtful thoughts. <br>2. Several loving acts or projects you can do for each person listed in the first column. | Set up (2) Columns. <br>1. Those people you tend to run down. <br>2. Listing several good characteristics and acts of each person can help you dispel hurtful thoughts. |

## Jesus and Self-Pity

When we allow self-pity into our lives, we will usually be concentrating on ourselves. The formula given by Paul in Romans 12:10 is "Be devoted to one another in brotherly love, Honor one another above yourselves." When self-pity descends upon us, we forget Paul's formula, and our view is turned inward.

Seeing Jesus's heart attitude when He was in the incredible physical, emotional and spiritual agony of the cross teaches us so much about how we should respond. Did He complain and gripe about His lot? Did He wonder aloud why His disciples had fled? Did he cry that the very ones He ministered to rejected Him? We would understand if He had, but He didn't. Instead, He made sure His mother was cared for. In the midst of His pain, He reached out. No whine of self-pity comes from Him. See how John records it,

"Near the cross of Jesus stood his mother, his mother's sister, Mary the wife of Clopas, and Mary of Magdala. When Jesus saw his mother there, and the disciple whom he loved standing nearby, he said to his mother, "Dear woman, here is your son," and to the disciple "here is your mother." From that time on, this disciple took her into his home." (John 19:25-27).

For those who might be struggling against this mighty foe, this might be helpful.

*(See chart on next page)*

# Applying Philippians 4:8 to Self-Pity

*Self-Pity is Dwelling on How Bad Events, People, and Circumstances are for You*

## R e p l a c e   W i t h . . .

| | Loving Thinking | Admirable Thinking | Excellent Thinking | Praiseworthy Thinking |
|---|---|---|---|---|
| **What to Do:** | Consider how you can give of yourself to someone. | Reflection on the good in others as opposed to faultfinding. | Meditating on how you can serve God and others better. | Thinking on the good God has done for me. |
| **How This Helps:** | When you begin to sink into ever-deepening levels of thinking how bad everything is, the cycle can be broken and turned around by acts of love and reaching out. | Self-pity is often marked by bad feelings of how bad others are to you, or even how bad I am. To see how good others are or even what God has done for me will change your outlook. | Bad self-image is often related to poor performance. It stands to reason that improved performance will improve one's view of self. | Ultimately self-pity focuses blame on God. Praise of God can properly re-align our thinking. |
| **Project:** | List the loving acts planned and completed. | 1. List all the good qualities and actions of anyone you can think of who has done evil towards you.<br>2. List all the talents, good personality traits, and physical features that God has given you that are good. | 1. List responsibilities and projects in Column 1 and methods of improvement in Column 2. | Rehearse what you are happy and thankful for. Make a list each day of all the things that God has for you. Should be related to specific events and circled as PTL's.** |

** PTL's - Praise the Lord!

A pastor was deeply discouraged. He was so full of despair that he went to the beach and wrote in the sand all the things he had against God. He prayed about all the terrible things written there and asked God to just take them. In the midst of the prayer, he felt what he described as a "tremendous presence." He opened his eyes in wonder and saw that the tide had come in and washed it all away.

## Jesus and Lustful Thinking

In his blasphemous attempt to bring Christ down to our level in The Last Temptation of Christ, Martin Scorcese pictures Jesus lustfully thinking of what it might have been like having sex with Mary Magdalene. As we have seen, Jesus Himself had already denounced such thinking as sin. Lust was something He simply did not do. In John 10:1-18, Jesus sets up His own giving attitude with the grabbing, self-centered robber and hired man. The robber sneaks in and takes. The hired man runs from the danger of the wolf, but Jesus gives His life for the sheep. Lust demands, "I want this for me." Love makes no demands and gives.

Bill Hybels comments,

> " 'I am not like a thief,' Jesus says. A burglar's basic aim is to break into your house and find something of great value that will get good money on the market. You hardly ever hear of a thief who makes off with four dishtowels, two throw rugs, and a tube of toothpaste; thieves look for jewelry, family heirlooms, paintings and electronic equipment. That's the character of a thief - to find what is precious and steal it."

What if Jesus had the attitude of a thief while on the cross? What if at that cataclysmic moment He had chosen

to demand His rights?  But He did none of these things.
He bore the sins of so many.  He died.  He gave His life for
the sheep.

   As we seek to practically put into place Jesus's attitude
regarding lust, let me suggest this diagram:


*(See chart on next page)*

# Applying Philippians 4:8 to Lustful Thinking

*Lustful Thinking - A Strong Desire for Something Material or Sexual*

**Replace With . . .**

| | True Thinking | Noble Thinking | Excellent Thinking | Pure Thinking | Praiseworthy Thinking |
|---|---|---|---|---|---|
| **What to Do:** | Thinking about things that are true as opposed to false and real as opposed to fake. | Concentration on what is important as opposed to what is trivial. | Thinking on how you can serve God and others with excellence. | Considering that which is uncontaminated. | Thinking on the good in God and what He has done for me. |
| **How This Helps:** | Since much lust involves fantasy (which isn't real), concentration on reality will replace lust. | Since most lustful thinking involves things that are relatively trivial to God, planning in the important areas of life will replace lust. | By putting our mental effort into plans for serving, little or no mental energy remains for lustful thoughts. | Filling my mind with thoughts of God can actually crowd out lust. | Since lust grows in the soil of discontentment, becoming more contented will retard growth of lust. |
| **Project:** | 1. Make a list of the major goals in your life.<br>2. What projects should you be doing now that will make progress in the achievement of one of these goals.<br>3. Plan out what you can do now in any of these projects. | | | Memorization of large passages of Scripture and review of passages memorized will replace lust. **Memorize:**<br>• Psalm 23<br>• 1 John 1,2,3<br>• 1 John 4,5 | Rehearse what you are thankful and happy for. Make a list of all the things that God has done for you each day. This should be related to specific events which should be listed and circled as PTL's. ** |

** PTL's - Praise the Lord!

As I seek to conclude, let me encourage you to do something about what you've read. The worst thing you could do (and I fear many *will* do) is to put this down, say, "that's nice," and go your way. The words of James 1:22 ring out a clear warning, "Do not merely listen to the word and so deceive yourselves. Do what it says."

There once was a man who, week after week, <u>ad infinitum, ad nauseum</u>, came to the back of his little church and shook hands with the pastor and said, "You really gave it to 'em, Pastor." Now the pastor realized that the man was missing the point. This man needed to listen and apply the rich teaching of God's word to his own life. But instead, he said, "You really gave it to 'em, Pastor."

One winter day, there was a huge snowstorm and all the roads were blocked. The parsonage was on one side of the church and the man's house on the other. At the appointed time, the pastor and the man were the only ones in the service. The pastor inwardly exulted, mentally threw away his prepared message and let fly with a message for his man. It was all directed at him. When it was over, the pastor went to the back of the sanctuary confident that the man would either accept or reject his clear presentation. Slowly the man got up and came toward the pastor. He stuck out his hand and said, "Boy, Pastor, if they had only been here, you *really* would have given it to 'em."

My hope is for better things for you. Apply Philippians 4:8 to your sinful thinking patterns. This is, in fact, an arena, but teamed up with the Holy Spirit and with the armor of God, ultimate victory is yours.

*Typography by:*

Paul G. Feith
COMPU-TECH CONSULTING


This book was typeset using MICROSOFT WORD FOR WINDOWS™ 2.0
and the LASERMASTER WINPRINTER 800™ Typesetter.

---